the new small house

the new small house

KATIE HUTCHISON

The Taunton Press

DEDICATION

For my parents, Joan and Bill Hutchison

The Taunton Press
Inspiration for hands-on living®

The Taunton Press, Inc.,
63 South Main Street
PO Box 5506
Newtown, CT 06470-5506
e-mail: tp@taunton.com

Editor: Peter Chapman
Copy Editor: Candace B. Levy
Jacket/Cover design: Sandra Salamony
Interior design and layout: Sandra Salamony
Illustrator: Katie Hutchison

The following names/manufacturers appearing in *The New Small House* are trademarks: 3form®, AstroTurf®, Azek®, Benjamin Moore®, Caesarstone®, Chilewich®, Corian®, Europly™, Forest Stewardship Council®, EGE®, Galvalume®, Gienow®, Glulam®, H Window®, HardiePanel®, HardiePlank®, HI-MACS®, IKEA®, Kynar®, Loewen®, Maax®, Mylar®, Polygal™, Rais®, Realtor®, Realtor.com®, Squak Mountain Stone™, TOTO®, Trex®, View-Master®

Library of Congress Cataloging-in-Publication Data

Hutchison, Katie.
  The new small house / Katie Hutchison.
      pages cm
  ISBN 978-1-63186-440-7 (hardcover) -- ISBN 978-1-62710-918-5 (paperback)
1. Small houses. I. Title.
  NA7533.H88 2015
  728'.37--dc23
                              2015022892

Printed in the United States of America
10 9 8 7 6 5 4 3 2 1

Katie Hutchison

ACKNOWLEDGMENTS

IT'S FUNNY how things work out. As I recall, some vocational test I took in high school informed me I should be an architect. At the time, I thought, "There must be some mistake; I'm going to be a writer." I blithely ignored the test, and off I went to be an English major and pursue a career in magazine publishing. But after working a short time as an editorial assistant for a magazine in New York City, I began to think, "Maybe I should be an architect." At age 23, I jumped tracks. I went to architecture school, eventually became an architect, and later established my own residential studio. Today, with this book, I have the good fortune to be both a writer and an architect. I am grateful to the many who supported me on my somewhat circuitous path, especially my parents, who have always believed in me.

I would also like to thank Chuck Miller, who gave me my first writing assignment at *Fine Homebuilding* magazine years ago and without whom *The New Small House* may not have come to be. And Peter Chapman, my editor at the Taunton Press, thank you for patiently considering my many book proposals over the years and for the clear vision you brought to guiding and shaping this book. Many thanks to the freelancers and the whole team at the Taunton Press who contributed their considerable talents and diligence to creating *The New Small House*. Thank you, as well, to Susie Middleton, who introduced me to the folks at the Taunton Press in the first place.

A heart-felt thank you to the homeowners and retreat owners (many of whom are also architects and/or designers) who so generously opened their small houses and retreats to the Taunton team and took the time to tell me their stories. You are a special group, living small deliberately and graciously. I commend you and the other architects, designers, students, teachers, builders, and tradespeople who helped craft the houses and retreats featured in the pages of this book.

And my dear husband, Chris, thank you for your patience, good humor, and sharing a small house with me. How lucky I am.

CONTENTS

INTRODUCTION

I LIVE IN A SMALL HOUSE in New England. My husband culled it from a stream of Realtor.com® listings for me to consider when we first began our house hunt while we were on vacation during a sultry July in 2012. This was a bit of a role reversal—for my husband to conduct the initial search—as I'm the residential architect in the family. But I was in full-on vacation mode that day away from the studio, and the real-world need to find a small roof to shelter us seemed a distant concern when just outside the window the beach beckoned, harbor breezes wafted, and the grill sizzled.

From the open living/dining area, the long view into the semiopen kitchen helps our small house feel larger. That's me sitting at the kitchen island.

So when I lazily pulled the laptop close to review his selections, the house that would become ours looked out at me from the screen much as a beloved pet might. It had locked eyes with my husband, too. He didn't say why, but he knew he'd found something special. I knew he had too, and I pondered the reasons.

Maybe it was the way the one-story ell presented its smallest face to the street almost coyly or how it and a close-by two-car garage shaped a side garden, deck, and clamshell driveway. Perhaps it was the oversize windows and raised ceiling in the open, shared living space. It might have been the daylight streaming through the southwestern nook, visible from within the north-facing kitchen. Or was it the warm southern yellow pine floors and the large limestone-like porcelain ceramic tiles that defined the kitchen and adjacent circulation path? Maybe it was the view across low windowsills in the living room, also seen from the kitchen, toward a break in dappled tree cover and the river beyond. It might have been the late-1940s narrow bead trim and diminutive crown molding that edged the windows and doors. Or was it the freshly painted original cabinets that lined a kitchen alcove,

which had been opened to accommodate a new kitchen island? Most likely it was all of these bundled into a small 1,550-sq.-ft. package that appeared to live larger than its modest size would suggest. Our instincts attracted us to our small house, and living in it today has only confirmed how well its expansive, versatile, sunlit design suits us.

We recognize good small-house design when we see it. But sometimes identifying why we like the small houses we like is more of a challenge. I'm here to help you meet that challenge, so ultimately you'll be able to shape the right small house for you. In this chapter, I'll share 10 fundamental design strategies for today's small houses (which I'm categorizing as 1,700 sq. ft. or less). Then, in later chapters—organized by water, country, village, and town locations—we'll explore how the design strategies are exhibited in 24 small North American houses. Some of the houses are newly constructed and others newly renovated. Most are primary residences for their occupants. We'll wrap up by considering how the same design strategies are portrayed by five small retreats (500 sq. ft. or less) on an even smaller scale in the backyard or beyond. Here we go.

WHY SMALL HOUSES?

On the heels of the recession there was a resurgence of interest in small houses and even smaller retreats. By 2007 the median U.S. new single-family house size had begun to shrink from 2,268 sq. ft. in 2006 to 2,227 sq. ft., and it continued to shrink through 2009 to 2,100 sq. ft. A confluence of economic factors, renewed environmentalism, and reconsidered priorities began to bring the small house back in favor.

Regrettably (and perhaps inevitably), in 2010 median new single-family house size began to increase again. Some theorize that's because those struggling with tight credit like first-time homebuyers, who typically purchase smaller houses (and bring down the overall median house size), have been pushed out of the market. In any case, the three-year spate of shrinking median new single-family house size caught the attention of many. In recent years, shelter magazines, newspapers, and blogs have been featuring smaller houses more and more frequently, and architects are displaying more of them on their websites.

I've chosen 1,700 sq. ft. as the threshold for small, though in 1970, that square footage would have been considered comfortably ample. I think you'll find that the houses featured here are indeed comfortably ample. In fact, the folks participating in the niche tiny-house movement—those who champion houses 500 sq. ft. and less—would find 1,700 sq. ft. downright extravagant. Of course, it's all relative, but for the sake of this book I've chosen not to focus on tiny houses. Norms change gradually, and I figure making the step from 2,300 sq. ft. to 1,700 sq. ft. may be an easier step for many to manage than the steeper drop to 300 sq. ft.

Despite the post-2009 return to increasing median new single-family house size, there seems to be a movement afoot among those who remember the lessons of the recession to live small deliberately. It's not only more affordable and gentler on the environment, but it can be empowering to have less to maintain, and less to worry about acquiring, less to distract from what matters, while still enjoying more of your time and more of the space you do have. To create a small house that graciously supports a simpler life, consider the whole-house (and whole-retreat) case studies on the ensuing pages, which demonstrate how 10 time-tested design strategies can be applied today.

Though our kitchen faces north, it borrows daylight and view from the open spaces it borders, which helps it feel less confining.

10 SMALL-HOUSE DESIGN STRATEGIES

If you've ever spent time in a small space, you're probably already aware of the challenges. A small space runs the risk of feeling cramped and confining. On the flip side, it can feel cozy, connected, and comfortable. Determining what factors contribute to each of those feelings can help determine how a design can avoid small-space drawbacks and enhance small-space assets. The 10 design strategies enumerated here aim to support an expansive, versatile, and well-crafted small house that relates well to its environment and natural forces.

These strategies are presented somewhat in the order you might address them as you begin your design process, starting from the broadest strokes and progressing to the finest lines. But, of course, the design process is fluid, and you might find yourself moving back and forth between a handful of the strategies or even getting an initial spark from the last strategy presented here.

1. BE SENSITIVE TO THE SITE

Your site may be your house's greatest asset. If your house is in the country or near a body of water, it may boast a significant natural feature or view. Organize your small house and outbuildings in relation to the natural feature or view. That may mean placing the house in sight of the natural feature without crowding it. Or it may suggest arranging your small house parallel to a wide view or in a way that frames an isolated view. Whether your house is located more remotely or is in a village or in town, place your small house so its relationship to other site elements or outbuildings shapes a rectangular outdoor room or series of outdoor rooms. Semicontained outdoor spaces can greatly expand small-house living area in temperate months. Incorporate hedges, pergolas, arbors, and fences to bound open edges and/or lead to site features. A small footprint will allow you to tread lightly on your property and to take advantage of its natural assets. Site the spaces in your house to capture natural daylight and augment or buffer its heat, depending on climate and season.

A lap pool and raised bed planters edge an outdoor room that fronts the small house beyond in this California compound.

The ceiling plane in this house on Lopez Island funnels northern light into the living space and compresses the horizontal view of the sea to the south.

2. PAY ATTENTION TO THE THIRD DIMENSION

Most folks who embark on the design of a small house begin by sketching a plan. Though the plan is a vital tool in conceiving how a small house is organized and flows, it represents only a two-dimensional view from above. But, of course, a small house is experienced three dimensionally from eye level. Considering the third (vertical) dimension is critical. Despite a small footprint, a soaring ceiling may lift our spirits, suggest a shared communal space, and allow for an additional function like a sleeping loft. A lowered ceiling or soffit may suggest a more intimate or task-oriented space within or bordering a taller space.

Just as the ceiling may be adjusted up or down, so can the floor plane. Stepped floor levels may differentiate a small space without dividing it. Even the height of elements on an exterior wall can significantly impact a small house. A windowsill 8 in. above the floor may feel less enclosing and, therefore, more expansive than a sill that's 3 ft. above the floor. Similarly, a window head that's 8 ft. above the floor may feel less enclosing and more expansive than a window head that's 7 ft. above the floor. Consider starting the design of your small house by sketching a vertical section (or vertical slice through your house), instead of the plan, in order to better take advantage of the third dimension.

Daylight from a large window in Ted Chapin and Torrence Boone's house washes down to the lower level thanks to an open bridge walkway. The distant view of Provincetown's Pilgrim Monument is visible from the upper level office and bridge.

3. BORROW DAYLIGHT AND VIEW

I'm convinced that people, like many plants, need abundant daylight to thrive. A small house should capture daylight where it can from multiple directions, and share it generously with the various spaces it contains. Open plans, ample windows, half-wall dividers, cased openings, and translucent or clear-glass paneled interior doors and partitions, to name a few features, allow daylight to travel more deeply into the interior of a house, enlivening and seemingly expanding what might otherwise feel like small, cramped spaces.

Similarly, views through one space to another and on to the exterior lend a sense of spaciousness. A borrowed view seen from the kitchen, across a dining space, through a living space, and out a window allows those in the kitchen to feel connected to the other spaces and outdoors, rather than hemmed in by tight walls. Cased openings, dropped beams over columns, and interior windows often lend order to open spaces, mark view thresholds, and can extend daylight and view.

4. MAKE A BIG STATEMENT

Just because a house is small doesn't mean everything in and on it should be small. In fact, a small house begs for some larger spaces, features, and furnishings. A small house that is primarily a single larger open room that uses low walls, soffits, and/or columns or posts to differentiate space (with perhaps one smaller room for a bathroom and some pockets for privacy) will generally feel more expansive than the same square footage carved into multiple smaller rooms. Likewise, a room with larger windows, on several sides, will likely feel more generous than one containing smaller windows punched into more enclosing walls, even if the windows are on more than one wall. A larger room with larger features can also comfortably accommodate some larger furnishings like a substantial chaise or beefy armchair and ottoman. Of course, if you overstuff a room—even if it's large—with swollen furniture, the room will start to feel cramped. It all comes down to balance.

The gang of windows and accompanying arbor at the entry to James Michelinie and Kyra Routon-Michelinie's Accessory Dwelling Unit in Portland, Oregon, makes a big statement on the relatively small gable end elevation.

 The living, dining, kitchen, and loft area all overlap at Trollstua Huset in Maine, taking advantage of an open layout with soaring ceilings.

5. CREATE MULTIPURPOSE SPACES

Spaces that are open to each other allow for overlap of function and greater flexibility. There simply isn't room in a small house to accommodate a different room for each activity or numerous hallways. Even opening a stairway with a more transparent or porous guard rail can add visual space to an adjacent living area.

Moveable elements like partitions or doors on tracks, cabinetry on wheels, and built-ins that fold furnishings into walls also allow spaces to be used for multiple purposes. Slide partitions open between sleeping alcoves and an adjacent central space to create a shared kids' playroom. Roll a kitchen island aside to make room for more leaves to be added to a dining table. Fold a bed into a wall to transform a bedroom into a living room. Multipurpose furnishings or millwork can spark a second use for a space. Try to provide for several activities for every area—like a stair landing that is also a window seat—to fully enjoy small-house versatility.

THE ICONS

To help you identify which of the 10 small-house design strategies are being implemented where, I've created an icon to represent each of them. Look for the icons throughout the book to see which specific strategies are at work. When each small house and retreat is introduced, you'll find a row of icons representing the strategies best exemplified by that particular house or retreat. You'll also notice icons in the photo captions. The more familiar you become with the design strategies and their icons, the easier it will be for you to identify how the strategies have been applied in the case studies and how to use them to your own small-house design.

 1. Be sensitive to the site

2. Pay attention to the third dimension

3. Borrow daylight and view

4. Make a big statement

5. Create multipurpose spaces

6. Shape pockets for privacy

7. Bring the indoors out and the outdoors in

8. Select a succinct finish palette

9. Invest in quality materials that matter

10. Design distinctive details that relate to the big picture

Ted Chapin designed this sunny pocket for privacy in an enclosed former front porch where activity on the nearby street and adjacent living area can be observed from a slight remove.

6. SHAPE POCKETS FOR PRIVACY

 While open spaces allow a small house to feel bigger, a small house that's too open can feel inhospitable. Most of us like to tuck aside occasionally to enjoy some quiet time while still in sight of shared, larger spaces. Populate the perimeter of open spaces with pockets for privacy where folks can sample some solitude without feeling left out of nearby activity. Window seats, desk alcoves, and/or inglenooks with overhead soffits or slightly dropped ceilings provide quiet moments to take a breath without missing anything. Pockets needn't be small, just smaller. A kitchen can be a pocket. A loft can be a pocket. Plan for pockets for peace of mind.

7. BRING THE INDOORS OUT AND THE OUTDOORS IN

 Create a sense of spaciousness by expanding your living area onto a deck, patio, and/or outdoor room. A sleeping porch, dining pavilion, or outside fireplace or fire pit all extend the indoors into the outdoors. Alternatively, create a sense of spaciousness by welcoming daylight and outdoor scenes deep into a small house with the aid of large windows, clerestory windows, transom windows, skylights, roof monitors, and/or interior courtyards that bring the outdoors in. Even something as simple as continuing a patio flooring material onto an adjacent kitchen floor or extending a wooden dining-area ceiling material out over intervening windows onto exterior eave soffits can stretch the indoor–outdoor boundary. Wicker chairs in a breakfast nook and an upholstered loveseat on an open-sided covered outdoor space can likewise delight and blur indoor–outdoor boundaries.

8. SELECT A SUCCINCT FINISH PALETTE

 Since much of a small house may be visible all at once, it's a good idea to reduce the palette of finish materials to a handful of elements that work well together. Perhaps the flooring is primarily one material and changes to another only under limited circumstances. Maybe it's wood most everywhere, including the kitchen and bathrooms, but stone tile at the entry and exit locations. Depending on the design of the house, this might mean a strip of large stone tile along an exterior wall of French doors or sliders, and wood flooring elsewhere. A succinct finish palette will help tie spaces together and allow them to read as a larger singular space rather than a cacophony of divided spaces.

Apply the same type of thinking to the interior paint palette. Choose perhaps one trim color to apply throughout the house and only one or two harmonious colors for walls and perhaps repeat a color or introduce a third on the ceilings. The continuity of your choices will allow discreet accents to pop rather than overwhelm.

 The dogtrot breezeway of this house on Lopez Island offers an opportunity to bring the dining experience outdoors and to bring the outdoors into the dining experience.

 The all-white board-and-batten exterior of the Old Acre Carriage House renovation by architect Gale Goff allows viewers to focus on the small house's charming form rather than be distracted by its component parts.

9. INVEST IN QUALITY MATERIALS THAT MATTER

 A small house often has a small budget, so choosing how to expend that budget is crucial. Invest in quality materials where they matter most to you without breaking the bank. Choose serviceable but more economical materials elsewhere. If your heart aches for the soft leather-like look and feel of soapstone counters, spring for them, but consider placing them atop affordable IKEA® base cabinets. If your idea of living is a clear-finished fir tongue-and-groove ceiling, consider it for your office alcove ceiling or on soffits above built-in window seats. But perhaps use fir overhead only sparingly as a beam treatment in the living space. Maybe faucets are your thing. Go ahead; get that deluxe rainmaker showerhead and high-design hand shower, but choose respectable, low-cost subway tile for the shower walls. Don't be afraid to mix high and medium quality; just avoid low quality. Apply the same thinking to your furnishings.

 It was important to Terry Ohm that quality materials like Monterey cypress and galvanized steel ceiling panels add warmth and texture, respectively, to his glass house in California. A solid-surface countertop of recycled material complements the palette without over extending Terry's budget.

The relationship of solid and void in the exterior window composition of Matt Kirkpatrick and Katherine Bovee's house is echoed in the composition of solid and void in the book cubby wall.

10. DESIGN DISTINCTIVE DETAILS THAT RELATE TO THE BIG PICTURE

One of the joys of designing a small house is the opportunity to express an idea through a big gesture and down to the smallest detail. Unlike larger, more complex houses, a small house can more easily communicate an integrated vision. It can be evident in a barnlike form of a house and its barnlike interior partitions, a minimalist exterior siding treatment paired with a minimalist interior finish detail, and an exterior window composition reflected in an interior cubby configuration. Imparting a bigger idea in a small detail lends a small house clarity. Details like a slatted wall finish, grooved planks that continue up an interior wall and onto a sloped ceiling, and book nooks punctuating a wall are most satisfying when they relate to the overall design. Distinctive details can make wonderful sense.

Of course, the 10 design strategies introduced here are interrelated. They work best in combination and are open to interpretation. In the following chapters, we'll explore how they can be combined and interpreted in a variety of small houses and retreats. Look to these examples for inspiration. Ultimately, imagine what you and your design professional can cook up by combining and interpreting the design strategies to suit your proclivities and specific situation. Sometimes you'll need to let your design simmer. It's an evolving process. Now that we've lived in our small house for a while, I have some new landscaping ideas percolating, so we can shape additional outdoor rooms and carve out secret-garden pockets for privacy.

With these 10 small-house design strategies in hand, however you combine and/or interpret them, you'll be better equipped to create a small house that informs and inspires the life you aim to live now and in the future. And when someone comes upon your small house and is smitten, you'll know why.

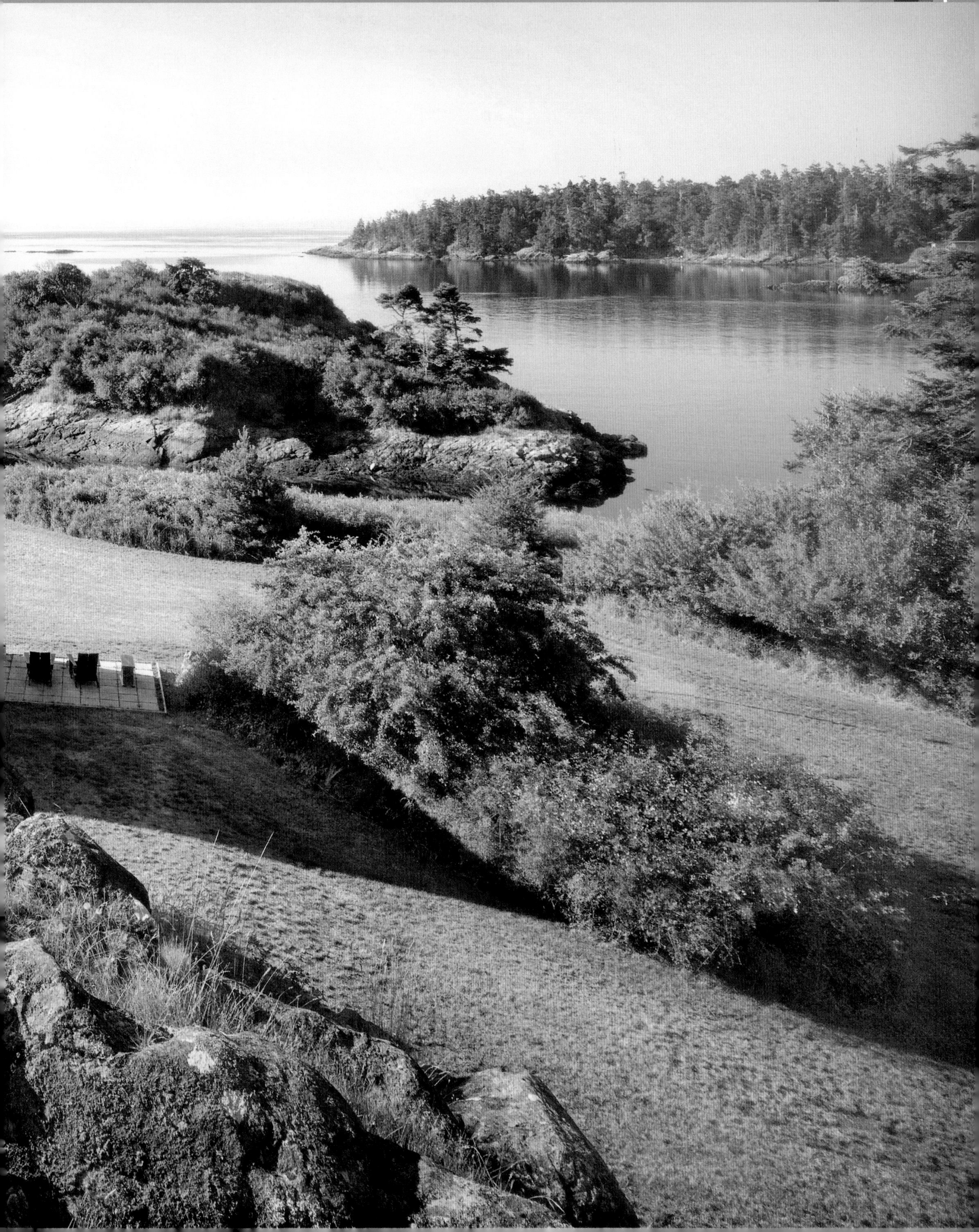

HERON COTTAGE

SITE 3D DAYLIGHT MULTI-PURPOSE PRIVACY IN/OUT FINISH PALETTE QUALITY MATERIALS

NOT MANY OF US have a chance to revisit with a fresh perspective a creative project we started a couple of decades beforehand. Architect Will Winkelman has enjoyed just such an opportunity. In 1990 as a young architect relatively new to Maine, he and his wife, Kathy Hanley, built a small cabin for themselves on property they acquired on Peaks Island. They named it Heron Cottage in reference to the great blue herons and night herons that frequent the unique site along a freshwater pond on one side and within view of the ocean on the other.

The cottage really does live sanely as a dwelling year round.

Tucked beneath trees and angled toward two views in opposite directions, Heron Cottage with its ample entry/entertaining deck takes full advantage of the site's multiple unique assets.

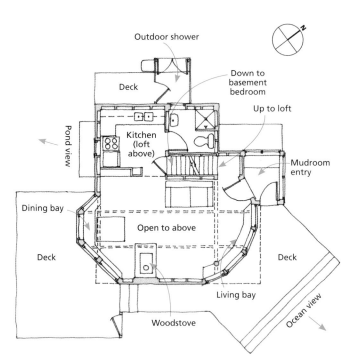

Outdoor shower

Deck

Down to basement bedroom

Up to loft

Pond view

Kitchen (loft above)

Mudroom entry

Dining bay

Open to above

Deck

Deck

Living bay

Ocean view

Woodstove

Architect: Will Winkelman of Winkelman Architecture

Peaks Island, Maine

600 sq. ft.

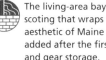 The living-area bay features galvanized corrugated steel wain-scoting that wraps the house and suits the rugged yet simple aesthetic of Maine retreats. A boxlike mudroom entry was added after the first summer storm necessitated more shelter and gear storage.

 The open dining/living area shares distant ocean views via the faceted bay. A birch tree that had been removed to make way for the cottage finds a new role inside supporting a beam. The woodstove flue climbs to exit through the roof instead of exiting via the side wall, so as much heat as possible is captured inside the cottage.

Their goal was to construct Heron Cottage quickly and affordably, so they would have a place to live on site while they designed and built what would later become the nearby main house. The cottage, they figured, would in short order transition into a guest house, a rental retreat, or accommodations for a family member. What they didn't anticipate was that the cottage would become their primary residence for seven or eight years while the main house design and construction percolated and was ultimately completed.

Fortunately, the cottage "really does live sanely as a dwelling year round," says Will.

Then a couple of years ago, Will and Kathy recognized that it was time to update some of the cottage's weather-worn materials and products. "To achieve the low-maintenance vocabulary, you have to spend some money," Will notes, and they were on a very tight budget when they originally constructed the cottage. While upgrading to extruded aluminum-clad windows, replacing the asphalt roofing in kind,

The dining bay borders a midlevel deck that enjoys views of the pond. Hefty eastern white cedar furnishings, handmade by Kathy, provide a comfortable spot to savor the surroundings. Galvanized corrugated steel makes another appearance to the left over the new bay window in the basement.

 The open cathedral ceiling is tall enough to accommodate a loft bedroom, which features a guardrail made of the same type of stainless-steel mesh that you might see around a bird enclosure. The ceiling is painted plywood to reflect light back down into the space. Hemlock ceiling battens tie the look back to the hemlock studs and board sheathing.

and replacing eastern white-cedar wall shingles and trim as necessary, Will tweaked the original design with knowledge gleaned from decades on the property and in the practice of designing homes. He left unchanged the many aspects of the design that had performed successfully over the years.

The original one-and-a-half-story design features a steeply pitched gable roof that's "evocative of Maine retreats, which are more traditional forms," according to Will. Taking advantage of the third dimension, a loft, open to the cathedral ceiling shared by the multipurpose dining/living space, is tucked in over the kitchen and full bath and provides a pocket for privacy. Two bays push out from a 14-ft. by 20-ft. core open space. One 45° bay off the dining area bulges to the southwest toward a view of wetlands and a freshwater pond, while another multifaceted bay off the living area reaches out to the northeast toward the yard and a distant view of the

 The dining bay is a cozy spot to enjoy the pond. Another birch tree, salvaged from when the house was constructed, is now a beam that spans between two rafter ties, providing a mounting surface for a pendant lamp above the table.

 The loft bedroom is easily accessed from a stair and offers a good siesta space for visitors who don't want to completely miss out on activity down below. A small peekaboo window provides a glimpse of the pond from the bed.

 The basement built-in bed and window writing surface contribute to the boat-like feel. Hemlock battens applied to hemlock boards imply a tree pattern in relief and add to the rustic Maine style.

ocean (allowing the dining and living areas to borrow view and daylight from opposite directions). Both bays include built-in benches that wrap double-hung windows. In the dining bay, a table efficiently nests into the window seat.

What the original cottage lacked was a truly habitable basement. "Before, you couldn't stand up in there," Will says. During the renovation, they dropped the basement floor, insulated with spray foam, improved drainage, and installed a bay window with a built-in writing surface looking out toward the pond. The new-and-improved basement bedroom with its wood ceiling is "like a ship's cabin," notes Will. Steps from the window desk is a Hobbit-size 5-ft.-tall door leading to a new private, red cedar deck and outdoor shower, which brings the indoors out and the outdoors in. Taking full advantage of the grade drop to the rear of the house, the renovated

private basement quarters, indoors and out, greatly enhance the cottage's livability.

Much of Will's other recent enhancements are more subtle but reinforce the intentions and strengths of the original design. A new guardrail system on the loft made of stainless-steel mesh and black plumbing pipe replaces the original cable guardrail, which Will decided was too techy for the cottage's rustic vibe. New hidden, low-voltage LED tape lights affixed to beams in the more enclosed spaces—like the kitchen, bathroom, and stairs—provide a welcome glow. A new closet door in the basement echoes a tree-like applied batten design also visible on a prerenovation access door.

Over the past quarter century or so, as Will has grown professionally and come to call Peaks Island home, Heron Cottage has grown to express his more complete vision for it.

With newly improved head height, the walk-out basement bedroom boasts its own private deck and outdoor shower.

The custom red cedar outdoor shower features shutters that the less shy can open to the view. The bench inside the shower extends to the exterior to serve as outdoor seating too.

MODERN VERNACULAR

SITE   3D   DAYLIGHT   BIG/SMALL   MULTI-PURPOSE   PRIVACY   IN/OUT   FINISH PALETTE   QUALITY MATERIALS

It looks like our house gave birth to a shed.

ARCHITECT BRIAN MACKAY-LYONS and the owners of this waterside home appreciate the local vernacular structures in and around Kingsburg, Nova Scotia. They chose a nearby barn as the inspiration for a new small house overlooking Kingsburg Pond and the Atlantic Ocean on a field that was once farmland. The house is a classic vernacular form, but reconceived using modern materials arranged in modern compositions to reflect a decidedly modern spatial sensibility.

 The cedar-shingled shed on the south end of the property acts as a foil to the modern-skinned house. The upper window in the double-height space on the gable end of the house is asymmetrical to enliven the composition (and also because there is a structural post occupying the center of the gable end that travels up to the ridge beam).

From the street, a large glass opening and adjacent sliding barn-style door announce the entry and make a big statement on the small house. Kingsburg Pond is visible beyond the house to the east.

The house occupies a modest 880-sq.-ft. footprint between the nearby street on one side and the view across the pond and out to the ocean on the other. The house and roof are clad in Galvalume® (steel sheet coated in an aluminum-zinc alloy), while a small gabled shed, by contrast, is cedar-shingled top to bottom. The shed is positioned to the south such that its east side aligns with the west side of the house, creating what Brian describes as a pinwheel dynamic, which shapes site-sensitive courtyards between the two. Brian notes, "We always try to put buildings on the edge of a site, so that leaves the site largely open . . . rather than plunking buildings in the middle of every field."

The choice of Galvalume on the exterior of the house and cedar shingles on the shed reflects the evolution of materials

Architect: MacKay-Lyons Sweetapple Architects
Kingsburg, N.S., Canada
1,400 sq. ft.

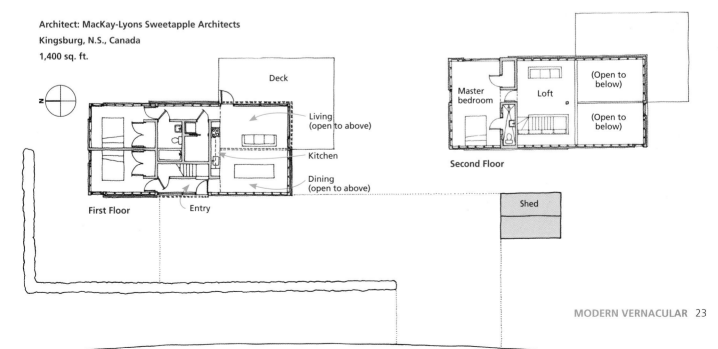

On the water and south sides, additional large glass openings give the corner of the house access to the view. The house's Galvalume walls and roof with tight eaves and barnlike wall apertures offer a modern take on the vernacular forms prevalent in the area.

 In the open, cathedral-ceilinged living/dining area, the diagonal tongue-and-groove board sheathing and exposed framing and fasteners contribute to the barn vibe. The lumber was milled at a local sawmill and sanded on site for a higher grade finish than exposed plywood sheathing.

The large corner window off the shared living space leads your eye across the pond and to the ocean in the distance. It both expands the living space outdoors and draws the outdoors into the living space. Structural sheathing and exposed beams frame the view in a warm wooden surround.

often seen on local barns as one skin has failed and been replaced by another. "What I tend to do is try to make the architecture of the outbuilding be the straight version or the traditional version, so it's kind of like a reminder of what the origin of this is," says Brian, referring to the inspiration for the house design. Granted, the shingled shed is itself an abstraction with only ½-in. eaves and an entry door clad in shingles. "It looks like our house gave birth to a shed," remarks the homeowner.

Three barn door–size openings create large voids on the otherwise mostly solid house elevations, making a big statement on the small house. Each opening is filled with large,

fixed, commercial-grade windows and smaller operable doors and/or windows. Choosing to use larger fixed window units rather than operable units to fill the openings is in keeping with the small house's small budget because fixed units are less expensive than operable units. Sliding hemlock barn doors are sized to cover the openings and can be closed to provide privacy, sun protection, and/or a safeguard from high winds. The oversize opening on the street side announces the entry, but because it fronts the narrow stair hall and faces a hill it doesn't overly expose the house to passersby. When the homeowners are away, they can slide the barn door over the entrance opening for additional privacy and security.

The kitchen opens onto the double-height dining/living space and shares the view and daylight. As with the other service core spaces, it's faced with economical Baltic birch plywood. Concrete counters echo the concrete floors, which are a cost-effective, functional, and aesthetic choice.

The stairs—also part of the service core—are lined with Baltic birch and edged with storage shelves to add depth and interest while maximizing function.

The loft study tucked under the rafters provides an intimate pocket for privacy that's open to the shared dining/living/kitchen space below.

The other two oversize openings are off the double-height open living/dining/kitchen space and face the eastern water view and southern sunlight. They "blow out the corner," as Brian puts it, in order to give the small house a sense of luxury and expansiveness, inviting the indoors out and outdoors in.

Inside, exposed framing, fasteners, and diagonal tongue-and-groove structural board sheathing on the exterior walls and roof continue the barn aesthetic. They are visible because the house is insulated on the outside (or *outsulated*) with rigid insulation rather than insulated between framing bays. Electrical conduits are cleverly concealed in the outsulation zone. The outside of the core service spaces of the kitchen, closets, bathrooms, and stairs are all finished in Baltic birch plywood, which helps organize and visually tie them together,

allowing one to easily flow into the next. Drywall makes a limited appearance on ceilings and surfaces that are not part of the exterior envelope or core. The first-floor concrete slab keeps costs down, is outfitted with radiant heat, and acts as a solar heat sink.

In a mere 1,400 sq. ft., the house boasts three bedrooms, a big study, and double-height living space. After entering the intimate and shallow cloakroom off the stairs beneath the second-floor loft, you proceed to the double-height expansive dining/living/kitchen area. "As you come into the house, it opens up, the full height of it, into one big room, and it frames the view nicely," says the homeowner. The dining and kitchen spaces borrow view and daylight from the large east- and south-facing corner windows off the living space, which provide a great sense of openness in a small house. A favorite

The deck wraps around the southeast corner of the house, extending living space outdoors. The placement of the shed suggests courtyard-like outdoor rooms between it and the house.

spot is the couch in the open living space, where the homeowners can enjoy panoramic views out the oversize windows. "You feel like you're sitting as an audience, and nature is putting on a performance," notes the homeowner. Upstairs, a loft study beneath the rafters provides a cozy pocket for privacy overlooking the open living area below, from which it borrows daylight and view.

"For a small house, you get quite a variety of experiences in it," the homeowner concludes. From its modern exterior to its warm textured interior, it benefits from a new small house interpretation of a tried-and-true barn form. Brian explains, "I say this is a prototype because it's in the language of a lot of the modest houses that we do; they're . . . almost invisible in the landscape."

LOW PROFILE, BOLD PRESENCE

| SITE | 3D | DAYLIGHT | BIG/ SMALL | MULTI- PURPOSE | PRIVACY | IN/OUT | FINISH PALETTE | QUALITY MATERIALS |

WHEN CAROL AND KEITH JAMES acquired their property on Lopez Island, Washington, the existing house was close to the bluff. Though they didn't keep that house, the footprint allowed them to site their new small house closer to the water than otherwise would have been permitted. But they didn't want to be too close. On the recommendation of their architects, John Eggleston and Allan Farkas, they placed the new house farther back and closer to an enormous outcrop. The architects positioned it up high enough to reach grade adjacent to the rock and for the view from within

If the budget is going to be tight, the solution has to be simple.

With its low-slope roof the house has a low profile in the landscape when seen from the water.

Architect: Eggleston|Farkas Architects
Lopez Island, Wash.
1,260 sq. ft.

Outcrop

Guest suite

Dogtrot breezeway

Kitchen

Master bedroom

Dining

Living   Woodstove

Deck

Views to water   Views to water

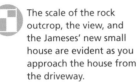

The scale of the rock outcrop, the view, and the Jameses' new small house are evident as you approach the house from the driveway.

From atop the rock, you get a good view of the dogtrot and guest suite, a small patio, nearby islands, and out toward the Strait of Juan de Fuca.

 The dogtrot is faced with vertical cedar tongue-and-groove boards—which also make an appearance on the interior walls—and the same ceramic floor tile as inside the main house and guest suite. The dogtrot frames the funneled view to dramatic effect and is sized to accommodate outdoor dining.

to clear a hedgerow along the bluff, yielding a better perspective of the nearby Richardson and Charles Islands and out toward the Strait of Juan de Fuca.

John and Allan designed a simple rectangular plan spanning a dogtrot breezeway, which separates a guest suite on the western end from the main house, and nestled the new small house sensitively into the rock outcrop parallel to both views: the rock to the north and the water to the south. For privacy from neighbors, the architects extended "blinders" on the east and west ends, the depth of a continuous south-facing cantilevered deck. They incorporated a simple low-slope roof,

pitched to the south in anticipation of future solar panels and to gather rainwater for a basement catchment system. "If the budget is going to be tight, the solution has to be simple," says John. And it helps that it's small. "It's cheaper. It's easier to take care of. Less maintenance," says Carol.

The materials and finishes of this minimalist house are decidedly new and succinct. The ends and top are wrapped with marine-grade, dark-bronze Kynar®-coated metal, while the south-facing wall sports full-height aluminum glass walls and sliders, periodically interrupted with vertical cedar tongue-and-groove siding with a light-gray stain. "I can't

imagine us living in anything but a fairly simple house, so it was the simple lines of it more than thinking we just wanted a modern-looking house," says Carol about what attracted her to the design. Those lines include the low-slope roof, about which John notes, "We wanted it to fit. So when you're out on a boat, looking back in at the site, that [the house] really sits as low as possible in the horizon, and you see the rock rise up behind it." The roof is sloped to channel rainwater into a series of holding tanks in the basement. "The projection for the island is that the fresh water table is going to decline and become less and less available through wells," says Keith. "It seemed to me that it would be prudent for us to have a backup system," he continues. From the exterior, that system is seamlessly integrated.

 Carol and Keith's house focuses the southern view through full-height glass, resulting in a form that makes a big statement for a small house (and is reminiscent of a child's View-Master®). The basement below is just tall enough to accommodate the sizeable rainwater catchment system and is accessed from double doors in the middle.

The open dining/living space enjoys a view through the sliding door system (made by Fleetwood Windows & Doors) to the narrow full-length deck and beyond, visually expanding the dining/living space out to sea and bringing the sea into the living space. A small Rais® woodstove warms the space without blocking the view.

You enter the house through the dogtrot breezeway, which frames stellar views in both directions, while bringing the indoors out and outdoors in. The breezeway provides some privacy for visitors in the guest suite, who even have their own laundry machines, as well as for Carol and Keith in the main house, while allowing both groups to overlap in the breezeway. The architects outfitted the ends of the dogtrot with sliding barn-style screen doors so the space can also act as a pocket-for-privacy sleeping porch for spillover guests.

Inside the main house, the kitchen, dining, and living areas share an efficient multipurpose space. The kitchen edges the rock-facing side of the space and the dining/living space edges the water side. Each borrows daylight and spectacular views from the other. The ceiling is flat on the water side over the dining/living area and slopes up over the kitchen area toward the rock. The effect of the change in the ceiling condition compresses the horizontal water view and then opens up to address the mammoth rock face. "We wanted to shut down the water side to prevailing storms," says John. "On the other

 Walnut-faced cabinetry and window mullions pick up on the rusty oranges in the rock outcrop and add warmth to the interior. Shelving built into the island cabinetry and facing the dining/living space provides versatile storage and helps the kitchen area feel less like a dedicated cooking area and more like part of the dining/living space.

 The flat ceiling on the water side of the multipurpose space and the sloped ceiling that climbs toward the rock on the opposite side allow for both a focused intimate view to the south and an expansive one to the north, providing a wide variety of experiences all within one space.

The master bedroom is just deep enough for a bed, circulation area, and built-in storage, all looking out to sea and accessible to the continuous water-side deck. The succinct finish palette of the shared multipurpose space makes an appearance here, too.

side, it faces north, and it's a good opportunity for us to bring in some nice tall north light into all those spaces back there," he continues. On both the north and south sides, the substantial amounts of glass blur the boundary between the house and the water, and between the house and the rock, bringing the indoors out and the outdoors in.

The interior and exterior color palettes overlap, and both were drawn from the colors of the site. The ceramic tile for the floors in the main house, guest house, and dogtrot, for example, echo colors found in the granite outcrop. Vertical tongue-and-groove cedar seen on the exterior relates to the site's trees and is the finish on the interior east and west end walls of the open kitchen/dining/living space too. "We actually really like to bring some of the exterior materials in the house and vice versa. It helps create this sense of indoor/outdoor space," says John. He continues, "Limiting the palette, also always helps with cost."

Carol and Keith's house projects a bold presence due to its hunkered steel and glass form hovering above a concrete foundation. It makes a big statement for a small house. But small it is. "It's very efficient. There's no added circulation. It's all on one floor, which works really well for an aging couple," notes John. It also works really well for a couple young at heart.

The narrow water-side deck features garapa, which wraps the floor, blinder ends, and ceiling soffit, echoing the treatment of the steel that wraps the sides and top of the house. A minimalist galvanized- and stainless-steel cable rail provides unfettered access to the view from this pocket for privacy.

ISLAND CHARM

SITE   DAYLIGHT   MULTI-PURPOSE   PRIVACY   IN/OUT   QUALITY MATERIALS

It's a different style of life over on Protection Island.

JOAN YOUNG HAS ALWAYS been interested in small houses. Her daughter, designer Sandi Cook, remembers that when she was growing up, her mom would sketch small one-room cabins and cottages on white typing paper as a pastime. There were reams of them. "It makes me wonder if that's where, somehow in the back of my mind, I got the interest in architecture," says Sandi. So when Joan decided to live in a small house she had purchased on Protection Island, a ten-minute ferry ride from Nanaimo, B.C., in Canada, she naturally teamed up with Sandi on designing the renovation.

 Passengers en route to or from the ferry often comment on the charm of the small red house with the periwinkle blue door offset by the even smaller shed and patio. Sandi added a minigable bracketed entry feature to better announce the entrance off the side.

The Dinghy Dock Pub and Restaurant runs a passenger ferry between Nanaimo and Protection Island, B.C., year-round.

They decided the 1960s house would need to be gutted down to the studs, but Joan had no desire to change the footprint or form of the house. Keeping it small was a priority. "I don't want to invest my time in a big mega-house with all the trimmings, that's not how I want to spend my money," she explains. And an addition or additions would have meant bringing more building materials and construction equipment to and from the island on a barge, which can get expensive and complicated. Instead, Joan invested in the house's existing shell and in patching the existing red cedar siding.

Reconfiguring window placement and choosing quality windows were important to her. She and Sandi opted for all new Gienow® vinyl casement windows, favoring their contemporary function, and, for a more traditional look, specified a cottage-style muntin pattern, which is often associated with double-hung windows where the upper sash is smaller than the lower sash. Depending on the window size, the advantage of the cottage style, beyond appearance, can be that the horizontal dividing muntin is above the line of sight when viewed from a seated position. Joan and Sandi debated whether to

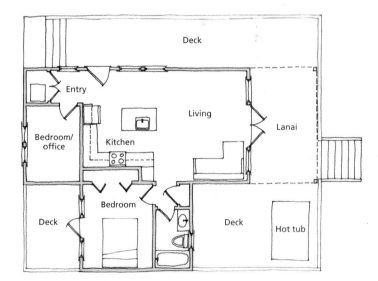

Designer: Sandra Cook of Tiro Design and Construction, LLC
Protection Island, Nanaimo, B.C., Canada
704 sq. ft.

divide the upper portion into three lites or six, and ultimately decided six would be too busy. They also saved room in the budget for a metal standing-seam roof, which is a common choice for long-lasting durability in their area. Air sealing and filling the shell's walls, ceilings, and floor with new fiberglass batt insulation and a vapor barrier made the house more comfortable for year-round living.

Inside, removing the existing wall between the kitchen and living area was critical to creating an open, multipurpose room. Sandi designed custom-painted cabinetry to neatly maximize storage and function and introduced a kitchen island with a wrap-around bar eating area to be used in lieu of a dining table. Joan selected wallpaper as a decorative and economical backsplash. Sandi notes, "You can always do whatever you want later," if, for instance, you decide someday that you want a tile backsplash or some other material.

Sandi proposed a large pair of out-swinging French doors (which take up less interior space than in-swinging doors) and

From the rear lawn, the lanai roof is visible. The shelter it offers lends the deck beneath it enough enclosure to feel at one with the adjacent interior living area.

In a small house with an open plan that flows well, nothing is ever far away or hard to reach. On the lanai and craving some lemonade? You're only steps from the refrigerator. Help yourself.

 The bamboo-topped kitchen island with sink and stool seating serves as prep and dining area as well as the centerpiece of not only the kitchen but also the living area. Custom kitchen cabinets painted Georgian green (Benjamin Moore®) and a HI-MACS® countertop from LG are purposeful and work well with the tone of the new oak floors.

 Upon entering the front door, the water view draws your eye across the open kitchen, through the living area, and out the French doors to the lanai. Sandi had the living area furnishings, mostly from IKEA, shipped to the Island on a barge.

PROTECTION ISLAND PARADISE

The 1960 Nanaimo Realty Co. promotion poster declares, "Escape to Pleasureful Protection Island!" and peddles 372 lots on what was to be "B.C.'s Newest Summer Paradise," complete with pirate theme. Today, the roughly 1½-mile-long by 1-mile-wide island is home to about 350 residents and is said to swell to 500 inhabitants or more in the summer. Frank Ney, the mastermind developer responsible for street names like Captain Morgans Boulevard, Captain Kidds Terrace, and Treasure Trail and park names like Long John Silver, Blackbeard, and Smugglers, later served as the charismatic long-time mayor of Nanaimo.

Folks rarely keep cars on the island. There are no gas stations, no grocery store, no movie theater. Residents travel the island by foot, bicycle, or licensed golf carts. "The roads all lead back to the same place," says Sandi. If you don't have your own boat for transportation, you go back and forth to Nanaimo—for supplies or to discard your garbage—on the ferry that's privately owned and run year-round by the Dinghy Dock Pub and Restaurant, the island's only commercial enterprise. In the summer, "Every hour there's a little parade of people either going to the ferry or coming from the ferry. Sometimes, they're just walking; sometimes they're

pushing wheelbarrows; sometimes they've gotten on their golf carts, or they're on their bikes," continues Sandi.

There is mail service to the island, a fire station served by volunteer firemen, a community center/library owned

by Nanaimo and leased by the Lion's Club, as well as a museum that recalls the island's coal-mining history. The island is considered a neighborhood of Nanaimo, and is, it would seem, a neighborhood like none other.

flanking fixed door panels, so the rear water view and breezes would be accessible from the kitchen island sink as well as to the living area sectional.

Because insects aren't nearly the problem on Protection Island that they can be elsewhere, screen doors weren't necessary. With the doors open, the rear deck, which nearly aligns with the interior floor level, expands the living area out beneath the rear roof extension onto what Sandi and Joan call

The lanai offers plenty of room for comfortable dining with the water view as a backdrop. Glass panels in the rear guard rail keep the view, when seated, unfettered.

 Joan decided to sink a two-person hot tub into the pressure-treated deck beyond the dining area, where it's both easily accessible but also not too prominent.

a lanai, bringing the indoors out and the outdoors in. During seasonable months, the family and guests enjoy all their meals at the lanai dining table. Together, the lanai and wrapping decks, bound by a guard rail, practically double the size of the living area in the summer.

Three small sheds on the property offer alternative future pockets for privacy, though they currently serve as on-site storage. The front shed houses a lawnmower and gardening equipment. The middle shed has a spare bunk in it, but it borders a noisy heat pump and thus is not an ideal spot for a siesta. The third shed at the rear to the northwest is quieter

and underused; Sandi imagines it may someday become a sweet bunkhouse. For now, the front sheds shape an appealing, site-sensitive outdoor space. Joan likes to park a chair out there or sit on the deck steps, holding court when folks are coming and going from the nearby ferry during the temperate months. "Every hour you can just go out there and sit, and you know, it's an island, so everyone waves to each other; you see people that you know," explains Sandi. "It's a different style of life over on Protection Island," notes Joan. Sounds like a dreamy one.

 A southeast-facing deck with an enclosing solid guard rail off the master bedroom provides a pocket for privacy for morning coffee and a view of passersby.

CAPE COD CASUAL

SITE 3D DAYLIGHT MULTI-PURPOSE PRIVACY IN/OUT FINISH PALETTE QUALITY MATERIALS

I'M A BIG FAN of outbuildings. I like the way they shape outdoor spaces, their informality, and how fun they can be to inhabit. So, naturally, I was taken with Cheryl Kyle's new small house on Cape Cod designed by Estes/Twombly Architects. It's a collection of small, low, gabled structures that run along a series of boardwalks and decks in which the outbuildings, at first glance, are difficult to distinguish from the main house. "The spaces between the different structures, when you spread it out like this, are as important as the structures themselves. So we're creating different

The spaces between . . . are as important as the structures themselves.

The kitchen and adjacent dining area borrow daylight and views from each other and are within conversational distance. Cheryl saved money by using birch IKEA kitchen cabinets, which she dressed up with 3form® Chroma countertops. The white-on-white interior palette and continuous bleached oak floors create a fresh beachy feel.

 The modest cedar-clad, one-story gabled buildings greet folks from the driveway and suggest informal Cape Cod beach living. "I wanted to echo the past with the shingles, but I wanted to bring it forward into this century," says Cheryl.

Architect: Estes/Twombly Architects
Brewster, Mass.
1,184 sq. ft.

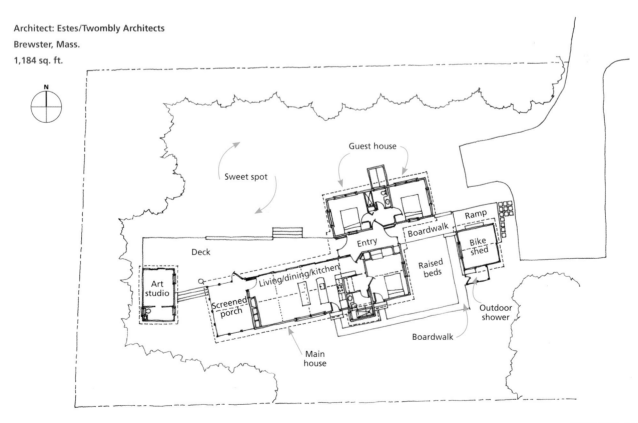

The deck slides past the bike shed to the left and approaches the screened entry between the main house to the left and the guest house to the right. The deck path and the garden it borders between the shed and main house both offer pockets for privacy in addition to providing an appealing entry sequence.

The boardwalk, entry deck, and buildings frame an outdoor room where Cheryl grows vegetables and herbs in raised beds.

The garapa deck off the main house kitchen/dining/living area and art studio edges the site's grassy sweet spot, inviting the outdoors in and the indoors out.

The screened connector between the main house and guest house provides some privacy separation while allowing the two to overlap easily in the summer months. In addition, the screen door indicates a threshold between the somewhat public entry sequence and the more private deck area off the shared kitchen/dining/living space, which leads to the art studio.

outdoor spaces as well as indoor spaces," explains architect Jim Estes. The informality of the arrangement harks back to the Cape Cod of sun-drenched memories, but it's designed for today's living.

A small bike shed on the east end of the property fronts the collection of small cedar-shingled buildings with standing-seam metal roofs. A ramp meets those arriving and leads past an outdoor room to the south, up along a two-bedroom guest house to the north, and into a screened-in enclosure between the guest house and main house. In the summer, the guest house and main house can both be open to the screen connector between them, which functions a bit like a dogtrot. Beyond the connector, a more private deck unfolds to the north of the main house's shared kitchen/dining/living space and leads to an unheated art studio on the west end.

"The layout of the buildings was geared toward the site, and I think every site has a sweet spot, where it's just a nice place to be or look at, and the sweet spot on this site is right below the main deck," says Jim. It's a relatively small grassy

The open kitchen/dining/living space and the screened porch beyond suit Cheryl well when she's alone in the house and are also generous enough in size and volume to comfortably accommodate visiting family and friends when she's entertaining.

The lofty screen porch at the end of the main house enjoys sun exposure on three sides and cross breezes. Its siting shapes an outdoor room or pocket for privacy reached by steps down to the south yard between it and the art studio.

area bordered by oaks and pines that's private from the street. In the winter, when the leaves are off, you can see beyond it to Cape Cod Bay. Cheryl's daughter, Camille Beehler, a landscape designer in Costa Mesa, Calif., created the landscape design of ornamental grasses and native plantings, which sets the stage for the sweet spot.

Cheryl enjoys having the spaces of the house divided among multiple structures because it allows her to live alone comfortably in the main house, with the guest quarters shut off or to accommodate a crowd during the temperate months, when she entertains family and friends, who can enjoy their own private space as well. "It goes through different phases at different seasons. When Cheryl's there alone, the main

part functions perfectly for her. Then in the summer, when the guests start coming, she gets a little distance from it," says Jim.

The 800-sq.-ft. main house is composed of a modest entry area with a flat ceiling that transitions to an open, multipurpose kitchen/dining/living area beneath an expansive cathedral ceiling. "In a small house, I think it's good to have some volume and space in the living area, so it can act like a bigger house when you have guests over," notes Jim. The multipurpose space shares daylight and views out the three sliding-glass doors that open onto the north-facing deck. "I love the way it's situated because you don't have this blinding light [shining] into your sliding glass doors," says Cheryl.

 Beneath an expansive wooden cathedral ceiling, like the one indoors, the porch feels very much part of the outdoor space yet connected to the main house by the sheltering roof and protective screening.

She and Jim chose a very simple white-on-white palette for the interior of the shared living area as well as the rest of the main house and guest house, which doesn't distract from the view outdoors and helps the spaces read as a continuous background for Cheryl's portrait and landscape paintings, collected objects, and furnishings. "I wanted clean and simple and kind of clutter free, but reflecting my travels around the world and my love of the Cape," explains Cheryl.

The western end of the kitchen/dining/living space opens onto the screened porch, which provides a pocket for privacy and additional outdoor living space. Just beyond the porch is Cheryl's art studio, another pocket for privacy. Over the past couple of years she's used the studio as additional special guest quarters in the summer and rolled her art-supply caddy onto the porch to paint there instead.

Cheryl's house is small in part to accommodate a tight budget, but also because small suits her. "It's just happier. People have to communicate; we have to all be together. We might have a puzzle going on the table and people running around and playing. I think small spaces are important and also spaces where, as in the guest house, you can get away from the rest," she concludes.

A skylight in the sloped ceiling washes the master bath in sunlight while preserving privacy. A modified IKEA cabinet topped with a 3form Chroma counter (which matches the kitchen countertop) serves as an economical vanity. A strip of 3form Chroma, matching the countertop, adds a hint of accent color to the shower walls.

SETTLED INTO THE LANDSCAPE

SITE   3D   DAYLIGHT   BIG/SMALL   MULTI-PURPOSE   PRIVACY   IN/OUT   FINISH PALETTE   QUALITY MATERIALS

Contemporary construction . . . that's comfortable to live in.

TROLLSTUA HUSET, which the homeowner loosely translates as Troll's Den in reference to Norway's mythical cave-dwelling trolls, was designed to replace a former failing ranch house. Regulations for the shoreland overlay zone in which the property is primarily located allow a new dwelling that's replacing a teardown to expand the floor area and volume by 30% each. This meant that a more conventional two-story home under a more steeply pitched roof would readily exhaust the volume limit. Plus, the stairs such a house would require would consume valuable floor area that could be put to better use elsewhere.

 Nestled between trees and oriented toward views of the river and sunlight, Trollstua Huset recalls the grass-roofed mountain dwellings of the homeowner's Norwegian heritage. "It's literally flowing nature on the building rather than placing it in nature," notes architect Will Winkelman.

 The southeast-facing patio fronts aluminum-clad double-glazed windows and double-glazed glass sliding doors with transoms above, which open to the river view and are topped by a twisting, soaring roofline.

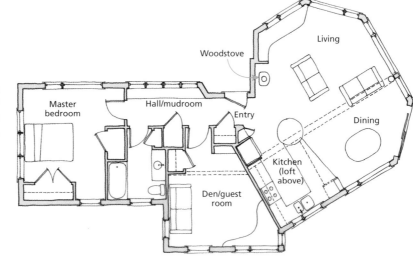

Architects: Will Winkelman and Eric Sokol of Winkelman Architecture
Brunswick, Maine
1,090 sq. ft.

Woodstove

Living

Master bedroom

Hall/mudroom

Entry

Dining

Kitchen (loft above)

Den/guest room

Instead, the architects suggested a collection of new one-story elements to house two bedrooms, a full bath, and an open kitchen/dining/living space with a loft to comfortably serve one resident and several overnight guests all within the regulated modest area and volume limit. They conceived of a roof that would start low and nearly flat toward the back over the more private bedrooms and gently rise toward the entry. Another roof over the combination kitchen/dining/living area would start at the height where the bedroom roof left off and then twist and rise more dramatically toward the best views and sunlight. This design causes the roofing material to be visible as you approach the house from the entry path, making a big statement on a small house.

The homeowner, who is of Norwegian descent, was familiar with grass roofs from her travels in the Scandinavian mountains and had grown to appreciate how they help settle

structures into the landscape. Will and project architect Eric Sokol recognized that planted roofs would be well suited to the twisting low-slope rooflines they had been proposing, which don't lend themselves as well to more conventional roofing materials. The team quickly realized that investing in quality planted roofs would recall the homeowner's Norwegian roots and address a number of issues: It would further insulate the high-performance building, manage runoff, and help integrate the house with the landscape. Chunky Maine-sourced tamarack siding and trim further tie the exterior to the natural environment.

In plan, the rooms tuck between existing oaks and white pines and are oriented toward the nearly 180° river view. "When we do space planning, we don't start with a box and figure out how the furniture would fit; we start with how furnishing would want to be arranged relative to the site, and then we build the walls around it," explains Will. It's a

Planted mostly with sedum and grasses that are prevalent around the house, the roof requires little maintenance other than the occasional weeding and planting of supplemental material. A hefty copper chimney anchors the entry and reflects warm tones and light as it vents the woodstove.

The 1-in. tamarack, a locally sourced material that's rot resistant and more affordable in long lengths than cedar, is arranged vertically, like wainscot, to suggest a base and then horizontally to emphasize the massing of the house and low-slope of the rafters. The 8-in. coursing relates to the wide trim dimensions on the eaves and is meant to reflect the rugged wood dimensions you find in nature.

The open kitchen/dining/living space is awash with daylight and mostly locally sourced materials. The exposed rafters are hemlock; the wall finish is eastern white pine; and the floor is slate, chosen for both its capacity to absorb passive solar gain and to transmit radiant heat.

A built-in ship's ladder (that does double duty on the back as shelving) provides access to the loft spillover space for guests like the homeowner's three nieces, while the lower ceiling formed by the loft creates a more intimate kitchen workspace. Cranberry-brown granite countertops complement the color of the slate floor.

The galley kitchen, complete with bar stools at the peninsula, is capped by a loft above, which is partially hung from an imposing steel beam. Beach stone knobs provide an organic contrast to clean-lined red birch cabinets here in the kitchen and also in the full bath.

The sloped spruce cathedral ceiling springs from the entry area just beyond the Danish woodstove, which has a soapstone finish and efficiently supplements the radiant floor heat system. A built-in desk provides an opportunity for privacy within the generous open kitchen/dining/living area while still providing a breathtaking view toward the river and its surrounds.

The front hall is a modest transitional zone cloaked in warm pine where the slate floor from the open kitchen/dining/living area is first introduced. A small niche with a built-in bench affords just enough room to sit down and take off your boots.

 The unique footprint of the den/guest room accommodates an organically shaped built-in corner desk with inspiring views through corner windows that bring the indoors out and the outdoors in.

site-sensitive approach that provides each of the primary spaces—the bedrooms and open kitchen/dining/living space—with views and daylight in three directions. "I stand in the kitchen while I'm cooking, and I see the whole landscape in front of me," says the homeowner, who from the peninsula counter enjoys borrowed views across the multipurpose open dining and living space. Even someone enjoying the pocket for privacy that the loft affords can share the view open to the common space below.

Though Trollstua Huset does appear to grow out of the ground as a cave opening might, the sense of light and airiness within is anything but cavelike. This is thanks in part to the form of the climbing cathedral ceiling over the multipurpose area. "The combination of the glass and wood and just the funky angles everywhere really gives it a more modern feel on the inside," notes the homeowner. An exposed steel beam supporting exposed long rafters, muted eastern white pine walls, a minimalist Danish woodstove, spare red birch cabinetry, and cable lighting further contribute to what Will describes as a "crisp crafted feel," which is also often associated with Scandinavian design. The homeowner adds,

"I wanted contemporary construction that was at the same time comfortable to live in."

Though site conditions and regulations largely influenced the total square footage and volume of Trollstua Huset, the homeowner concludes, "I've been pleasantly surprised at how perfect the size is for me. I think that is attributed to the way that the space has been allocated." It also easily accommodates her visiting extended family of seven, in addition to her vast collection of Norwegian trolls.

RESIDENT GUESTHOUSE

| SITE | 3D | DAYLIGHT | BIG/SMALL | MULTI-PURPOSE | IN/OUT | FINISH PALETTE | QUALITY MATERIALS | DETAILS |

You almost feel like you're camping out.

SOMETIMES FOLKS SAVE the best towels and sheets for their guests or maybe the best seats at the table. Sometimes guests even get the best accommodations, the fun digs in the attic or out back in a separate retreat. And sometimes switching places with a guest may look like a desirable alternative. Architect John Carney and his wife, Elaine, decided to step into their guests' shoes—their future guests' shoes. They designed a guest house for themselves on 5 acres of woodlands in Wilson, Wyo., while plans and funding for their future main house there were brewing. Local zoning requires that guest houses be no larger than 1,000 sq. ft.

When approached from the south, the garage and house frame an entry deck area among boulders found on site and a few of the trees that appear in abundance in the surrounding Wyoming woods.

From the southern sunny deck you can see clear through the open kitchen/dining/living space to the northern deck and vice versa, extending living space into the site in both directions.

The garage and small house are placed in close proximity because of Wyoming's often inclement weather. John chose to clad the entire garage in bonderized steel panels—oriented horizontally to differentiate it from the vertical treatment on the house—and eliminate the roof overhang there so as not to compete with the house. The two shed forms are in harmonious, simpatico dialogue.

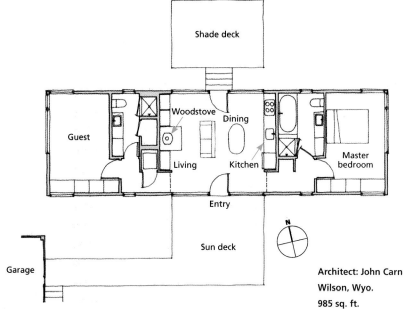

Shade deck

Woodstove   Dining

Guest

Living   Kitchen

Master bedroom

Entry

Sun deck

N

Garage

Architect: John Carney of Carney Logan Burke Architects
Wilson, Wyo.
985 sq. ft.

When seated on the couch facing the TV, bookshelves, and the Rais woodstove, you can glance left or right to enjoy broad views across the property into the woods.

At 985 sq. ft. John and Elaine's guest house, temporarily turned small primary residence, is a study in contemporary sophisticated simplicity in siting, plan, form, and material.

Sited on an east–west axis roughly parallel to a creek on the north side, the narrow house spans across the contours of the wooded property, with the east end facing downhill and the west end looking uphill at the site of the future main house. Sensitive to the site, John and Elaine wanted to take full advantage of the property's natural features and the sun's daily path. "The whole idea is a very transparent middle of the building, which is about 20 ft. of the full 58-ft. length, and that is glass on both sides," says John. From the multipurpose open kitchen/dining/living space you can look out the large

expanse of glass on the sunny side at arriving guests or turn toward matching windows on the shady side to savor the view of the creek, bringing the outdoors in; better yet, in just a few steps, you can dine or lounge on the sunny or shady deck, bringing the indoors out.

The east and west ends of the house, which each contain a bedroom, feature sizable corner windows by Loewen® that extend all the way to the floor. Because the corner windows admit daylight and view from two directions simultaneously, they feel more expansive than separate windows placed within the same walls would. "You almost feel like you're camping out, that you're in the woods because the room is small and your toes are almost outside," notes John. Yet the Carneys are

 The kitchen edges one wall of the open space and accommodates all of the appliances, storage, and work space within its 12-ft. length. The Heath Ceramics subway tile backsplash runs vertically, a subtle echo of the bonderized steel and shingle pattern on the exterior.

Corner windows that extend to the floor minimize the barrier between inside and out, making each feel like part of the other. Fortunately, the glass does keep the bears and moose at bay.

happy the glass prevents the outdoors from literally coming in: They once spotted a black bear outside their bedroom window gnawing on the glass.

John and Elaine selected the eastern room as the master bedroom because they love the morning light. The western bedroom is a mirror image in plan, but they've furnished it as a study with John's desk and a day bed. One of the perks of the mostly symmetrical plan is that the room use/designation is flexible because there are two spaces of the same mirrored size and configuration. Both bedrooms contain built-in millwork closets and a built-in bureau with a window above rather than closets framed with space-consuming studs and a freestanding bureau that takes up floor area.

A simple shed-roofed form seemed a natural choice for the house and nearby garage. John toyed with a gable roof early in the design process, but the shed won out, in part,

because of its practicality. He chose significant overhangs to shelter the house from harsh sun and weather. The upper eaves extend 5½ ft.; the lower eaves extend just over 4 ft., and the rakes extend 4 ft. John worked with his engineer to design a steel T-section, which they call a structural fascia, to support the shallow framing across the significant overhangs. The resulting prominent roof resembles the mortarboard of a tipped graduation cap and makes a big statement on their small house. Inside, you experience the gentle sloping shed roof in the cathedral ceiling of all the spaces except the bathrooms.

Also notable on John and Elaine's house is the unique and limited palette of materials and color. John selected bonderized steel panels as an accent on the house and for the complete exterior of the garage, in part because it isn't flammable, and their property is in a fire-hazard zone. The majority of

 The corner windows in the western bedroom welcome afternoon light into the room that John and Elaine have furnished as a quiet study and sitting area.

 From slightly up hill to the west, you can see the shady deck and the matching slopes of the shed roofs—angled at the house to capture southern sun and drain toward the creek. The large corner windows and overhangs make a big statement on the end elevation of the small house.

the siding is treated noncombustible shingles, which complement the wooded site. On the house, the bonderized steel steps down to meet the heads of the windows and doors, while the shingles project past the heads of the windows and doors; the materials visually engage or lock together and create a distinctive detail of woven vertical elements. The roofs on both the house and the garage are corrugated bonderized steel. Inside the open multipurpose space, white-washed white oak floors and cabinets team with an all-white paint palette on the walls and ceilings to streamline the look. With an eye toward a succinct finish palette, John notes, "If I can do a house with two or three materials that to me is Nirvana."

Indeed, it's quite possible John has achieved a small slice of Nirvana in the woods of Wyoming. Soon he and Elaine will move up to the main house, leaving the guest house for visitors. So now I'm wondering how I can get on the guest list.

John introduced vertical bonderized steel panels to break up the scale of the house. The panels extend down to the window head, while the shingles extend past, creating vertical panels of shingles as well. "We like the interweaving of the two materials," notes John.

PASSION FOR PASSIVE

SITE 3D DAYLIGHT BIG/SMALL MULTI-PURPOSE PRIVACY IN/OUT FINISH PALETTE QUALITY MATERIALS DETAILS

"I AM NOT A COOK," explains Wendy Everham. Neither is her husband Bill. "If there was anything that I would do over again, to the horror of my friends and family, I would have made the kitchen smaller," she laughs. This is the mind-set Wendy brought to the design of her space-saving, energy-efficient new house in Bath, Maine, which she developed with GO Logic from one of their concept plans.

I'm absolutely using every inch of the space that I have.

The gang of three door-size front windows creates the illusion of one extra-large window, in part due to the shingle flare above. The cutout for the front porch provides another substantial opening to balance the large window gang. Together, the oversize openings in the diminutive gable and shed form make a big statement.

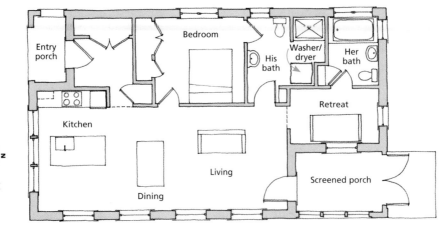

Architect: GO Logic, LLC
Bath, Maine
1,000 sq. ft.

Just as the eaves provide a brim for the roof, the shingle flare provides a brim for the gang of oversize windows.

"I've always been interested in sustainable living issues," notes Wendy, who is a naturalist, and appreciated that a small footprint, sensitive to her wooded site on a knoll, would be the first step toward a sustainable and affordable house. "I was very intrigued by this concept of a passive house: a very well-insulated house, using fewer natural resources for heating and cooling," she continues. That interest led her to architect Matt O'Malia of GO Logic via the Passive House Institute U.S. (PHIUS).

She also knew that she and her husband would want a fair amount of privacy in their small house and that a one-story house in which they could retire would mean there would be no escaping to the second floor for quiet time if need be. She and her architect noodled around with a GO Logic concept plan that was a simple rectangle, a form that is economical and efficient to build, insulate, and condition; it included a multipurpose open kitchen/dining/living area with a 9-ft.-high ceiling, in which spaces open directly onto one another rather than off space-eating hallways. Around the shared common area, they carved out a private bedroom and two bathrooms as well as intimate pockets for privacy for a retreat spot, rear screened porch, and front entry porch, all with lower ceilings.

From the inside, the front tall windows read more like a window wall, drawing the woods inside. Soapstone counters, white oak floors, and custom white oak cabinets add warmth to the bone-white wall and dove-white trim palette.

 The inset front porch is large enough to provide some shade for a rocker and shelter for those entering

Wendy's tidy white bathroom sports a Maax® soaking tub and a space-saving TOTO® pedestal sink. The wainscot is a plain-spoken splurge.

The two full baths were a splurge she and Bill preferred to a more conventional second bedroom in place of the retreat space and second full bath. "We've been married for a long, long time . . . I love baths; he likes showers. I like a neat bathroom; he doesn't really care," says Wendy. Her bath features a deep soaking tub. His contains a generous shower and a stackable washer/dryer. The retreat space accommodates a day bed and might alternatively include a desk someday; in which case, the day bed would move out to the common space, which is a flexible multipurpose area. A consistent palette of muted whites contributes to that versatility and allows the view of the woods beyond to pop by contrast. Wendy remarks, "It's a big open space, and I can pretty much do whatever I want with it."

One thing she didn't want to do with it was fill it up with kitchen equipment and cabinetry. There's no oven, no dishwasher, no microwave, and only one overhead cabinet. Instead, she opened the house to the outdoors with large windows featuring low sills, paying attention to the third dimension to maximize view and daylight. By keeping the majority of the south wall cabinetry free, Wendy and Matt recognized that they could introduce substantial south-facing windows to increase passive solar gain. From the exterior, the 3-ft. 3-in. by 7-ft. 6-in. windows make a big statement on the modest front gable. On the inside, they wash the common living space with daylight and enhance the connection to the woods, bringing the indoors out and the outdoors in. The regularly spaced east-facing windows are also large

 The modest kitchen serves Wendy and Bill's day-to-day needs but wouldn't be considered a cook's kitchen.

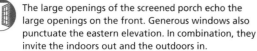 The large openings of the screened porch echo the large openings on the front. Generous windows also punctuate the eastern elevation. In combination, they invite the indoors out and the outdoors in.

(3 ft. 10 in. by 6 ft. 6 in.) but not quite as tall as the gang of three south-facing windows.

GO Logic provided the triple-glazed, tilt/turn German windows by EGE® for Wendy's local design/build project, and they generally also provide windows manufactured by EGE for projects further afield where GO Logic is retained as the architect but not the builder. Matt sees the windows as a key part of the high-performance package GO Logic delivers. Though Wendy and Bill's house is not certified as a passive house, it includes an 80% to 90% efficient energy–recovery ventilator and R-50 wall assemblies constructed of 8-in. structural insulated panels (SIPs) and interior 2×4s filled with dense-pack cellulose. R-80 ceilings are obtained with 24 in. of dense-pack cellulose on the floor of the attic trusses, and an R-60 foundation is achieved with 12 in. of expanded

 A sizable rear landing turned mini-deck provides a perch to survey the woods.

Triple-glazed German tilt/turn windows invite summer breezes when open but keep winter winds at bay when closed. Their thicker frames are in proportion with the home's thicker walls. The long view through the screened porch is visible from the kitchen.

THE EUROPEAN TILT/TURN ADVANTAGE

Matt O'Malia likes to say, "Passive House was invented in the U.S. and refined by the Germans." The way he sees it, the movement in the 1970s in the United States, which is known for touting passive solar energy, also sparked considerable interest in super-insulated buildings. However, one of the significant weak links in the original U.S. passive solar movement was the windows. They were un-insulated, single-glazed, poor performers.

Enter German engineer-ing. Today, triple-glazed tilt/turn windows are the norm in the German market. Not so much in North America. Matt will grant that the climate most Germans share is differ-ent from the climate range in North America, where the window performance required in chilly Minnesota is not the same as in balmy Florida. For his projects in cold-climate Maine, he imports tilt/turn windows directly from EGE in Germany.

Wendy and Bill's windows are aluminum clad on the exterior and painted wood on the interior.

Unlike double-hung win-dows, tilt/turn windows can be air sealed. They tilt in from the top (like hopper windows) to provide ventilation, or, alternatively, they turn (like in-swinging casements) to provide egress or more ven-tilation. With the turn opera-tion, the windows can easily be cleaned, inside and out, and the screens can readily be clipped to the exterior from the interior. The tilt function also acts as a security feature, and, if inadvertently left open during a driving, horizontal rain storm, the tilt function prevents adjacent furniture from getting soaked. "From a security and venting stand-point, the tilt/turn is really quite handy, and then from egress, cleaning, and main-tenance, they're great," con-cludes Matt.

The screened porch provides a great alternative dining or working spot in seasonable weather as well as a pocket for privacy. "We live on that porch most of the time," notes Wendy.

polystyrene (EPS) foam under the nonthickened portion of the slab.

Wendy is pleased with her new house's spatial and energy efficiency. "I'm absolutely using every inch of the space that I have, so nothing is wasted. I'm not heating a room that I never go into. I'm not paying taxes on a room that I'm not using," she says. And, she notes, "A great deal of our delight with the house has been the mechanics of it." Wendy and Bill lost power for 24 hours one February due to high winds, but they lost only one degree of heat in that time. Making rigorous choices about how much they need, and how to insulate and condition what they need, has yielded the ideal house for Wendy and Bill. "This, of course, is not for everybody, but it did work just fine for us," she concludes.

BARNHOUSE MODERN

SITE

3D

DAYLIGHT

BIG/SMALL

MULTI-PURPOSE

PRIVACY

IN/OUT

FINISH PALETTE

QUALITY MATERIALS

DETAILS

It's definitely a house designed for a couple.

AFTER FOUR YEARS of periodically camping on their 55-acre farmland in southeastern Iowa, Geoff and Joanna Mouming became well acquainted with their property and the type of house that might suit their life there. "We like modern. We want to respect the context. We like vernacular buildings in Iowa," says Geoff. And, Joanna adds, "We like each other quite a bit, so we like to live closely." With the general criteria established, they contacted John DeForest of Seattle, a like-minded architect, to help them envision a new, modern interpretation of a barn for their small house in America's Corn Belt.

Architect John DeForest designed a simple vernacular-inspired form with barn-red board-and-batten siding on the central section and timber-frame shed components for the entry porch and porch-like dining area. High-performance double-glazed H Window® units hint that this is not your grandfather's farmhouse.

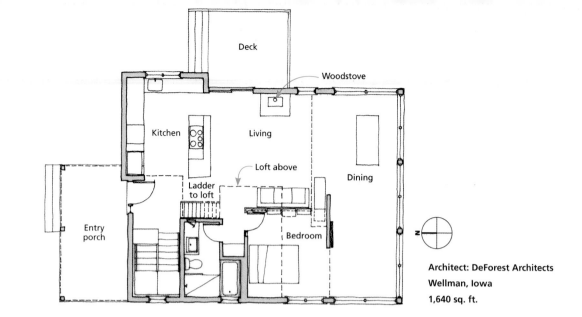

Deck

Woodstove

Kitchen

Living

Loft above

Dining

Ladder
to loft

Entry
porch

Bedroom

N

Architect: DeForest Architects
Wellman, Iowa
1,640 sq. ft.

Together, the three of them decided to site the house near the top of a gentle slope, so they would be able to overlook the gardens they planned for the yard and the acreage of former farmland they hoped to restore (as much as possible) to native prairie. Because they aim to grow old on the property, Geoff and Joanna decided the majority of the living space would need to be close to ground level, but they liked the idea of a modest walk-out basement where they would have easy access to their gardens below. In a book, they found a floor plan for a small lakeside cabin, which included front and back porches, and shared it with John as a design starting point.

After gathering some vernacular barn images and Grant Wood's painting *Young Corn* for inspiration, John sketched a simple form reminiscent of a barnlike farmhouse. Red board-and-batten siding on the main central volume is flanked by two porchlike shed wings—one offering entry and the other sheltering a small walk-out basement below—that reach north and south, respectively. From the exterior it reads more vernacular than modern, but step through the flush Dutch door and the balance shifts.

Geoff and Joanna splurged on lapped cedar siding for the kitchen bump-out as well as a galvanized metal standing-seam roof, but made budget decisions about other material selections. The eastern deck, just steps from the kitchen and their gardens, provides an alternative dining spot.

 Expansive views out across the yard and pastures are open to the multipurpose living space beneath maple plywood projecting flat ceilings and the cathedral ceiling that peaks at around 19 ft.

The living area borders the slatted corncrib-inspired partial wall of the bedroom. Just beyond, lays the niche for the TV cart. Reclaimed Douglas fir floors balance the warmth of the maple plywood ceiling treatment, which suggests a fresh take on barn board sheathing.

The first floor is a mostly open multipurpose space, with the exception of the full bathroom. One space blends into another, often in unexpected ways. An 8-ft. flat ceiling of maple plywood strips greets you at the entry and draws you into the greater space beneath a cathedral ceiling of the same material. Ahead, is a ladder leading to a loft, which partially overhangs the living area couch and a slatted wall that borders the bedroom. Beyond, in the space that from the exterior resembles an enclosed porch, a stretch of windows looks south beneath another projecting, flat 8-ft. ceiling of maple plywood strips.

Distinctive details that recall barn elements reinvent those same elements with a fresh contemporary twist. The exposed loft joists, for example, suggest the open framing of an overhead haymow. This one, however, serves as a home office pocket for privacy bound by a light-sharing translucent partial wall like no haymow I've ever seen. The slatted partition between the bedroom and living space is a play off the idea of a corncrib. Light peeks through the gaps between the boards, but people can't because the gap between the boards is at a 45° angle. On the bedroom side of the slatted partition, moveable storage cubbies hang from the angle-cut slats.

The "dining porch," as Geoff and Joanna call it, extends to the end of their partially open bedroom, which features Chilewich® panels that they can slide close for some privacy when they have house guests.

Similar deeper cubbies provide openings through the partition that allow the living area to borrow western light and view from the bedroom and the bedroom to borrow eastern light and view from the living area.

In fact, the bedroom is porous in other ways, too. The slatted wall doesn't fully enclose it. A gap between the end of the slatted wall and the perpendicular partial wall provides a slot for a TV media cart that can roll into the living room or the bedroom depending on where Geoff and Joanna want to watch. In a small house, this kind of double-duty multi-purpose solution means there's no need for two TVs only feet apart separated by a partition. Because the loft doesn't fully cover the bedroom and the south wall of the bedroom doesn't extend all of the way across, Geoff and Joanna can enjoy southern light from the porch-like space and connection to the greater space contained by the cathedral ceiling. To re-interpret the look of board sheathing on a barn, the 16-in. by

The bedroom's slatted partition accommodates storage cubbies that can be relocated as necessary. (Geoff and Joanna have a walk-in clothes closet in the basement; because it's a small house, that isn't far away.) Part of their bed lays beneath the haymow-like loft, while the rest is open to the cathedral ceiling of the open living space.

 From the loft workspace, you can savor the view of the valley beyond. Translucent twin-wall polycarbonate horticultural plastic (commonly used for greenhouses) on the low loft wall is an inexpensive way to share light between spaces.

8-ft. maple plywood strips on the ceiling were applied with spaces in between over a drywall ceiling that was painted black and is yet another distinctive detail.

Because the bedroom is only partially enclosed, it's very much part of the open living/dining/kitchen and, as such, is more inviting than if it had been a closed-off tiny space within a small space. Bringing the bedroom into the common open space of the living/dining/kitchen is a big statement in a small house. "It's definitely a house designed for a couple," says Geoff. "We can flow in and out pretty comfortably," he continues. That movement includes visually flowing out to the landscape they cherish via expansive windows and physically flowing out through the eastern deck, entry porch, or walk-out basement. "We wanted it to spill outdoors," notes Joanna. They also wanted to shape a home that uniquely reflects the way they live. And so it does. "It was a way to express something that we probably didn't know was within us," concludes Geoff.

The freestanding entry-area wardrobe features the same Europly door fronts and cutouts as the kitchen cabinets. The red sidewall made from FinnForm (used for concrete forms) is the same economical material used for the ladder stringers and inside the through-wall cubbies between the bedroom and living space. An inventive rolling bench/drawer stows snuggly within the wardrobe.

An avid cook, Joanna opted for a full wall of kitchen storage so there would be room for everything. The maple Europly™ cabinet fronts sport cutouts instead of hardware pulls for a playful touch. Visiting children like to place little dolls and figurines in them.

Galvanized corrugated metal faces the shower wall and serves as another reinterpreted agrarian reference. A salvaged work sink that once served as a planter at Geoff and Joanna's previous residence finds yet another life (once resurfaced) as the master bathroom sink atop a simple angle-iron stand.

LONGHOUSE

SITE 3D DAYLIGHT BIG/ SMALL MULTI- PURPOSE PRIVACY IN/OUT FINISH PALETTE QUALITY MATERIALS

ONE OF THE SIMPLEST, most economical forms for a small house is a rectangle or long bar. Generally only one room wide, the beauty of the bar house is the simplicity of its long footprint, the potential for daylight penetration and ventilation across its short dimension, and the opportunity for wide vistas along its long dimensions.

Native Americans referred to this type of form as a longhouse. Architect Eric Reinholdt became familiar with the Native American longhouse as a frequent childhood visitor to the North American Indian

> We wanted to be able to capture light on both sides equally.

Clad in affordable white HardiePlank® lap siding and topped with practical Galvalume-coated steel—the roofing material of choice for Maine's agrarian buildings—the white and silver longhouse is reminiscent of the fallen birches it replaced.

art and artifacts exhibitions at the Fenimore Art Museum in Cooperstown, N.Y., where his father was the director of education for the New York State Historical Association. The longhouse in Native American culture sheltered multiple families in communal spaces under one roof. Reinholdt isn't of Native American descent. He has some German and Norwegian roots, and it just so happens that the longhouse is also a form found in medieval Germany and Norway. The European version sheltered family living quarters and barn activity all beneath a common roof. "It was always part of my internal consciousness, the longhouse form," says Eric.

He liked the idea of adapting a longhouse, with its communal spaces, into a small economical house for his young family of four—his own small community. He and his wife, Laura, found an affordable 4-acre lot on Mount Desert Island, Maine, 3½ acres of which were wetlands. The ½ acre of buildable area on the lot was partially covered by a swath of fallen birches, which inspired Eric's siting of his white fallen birch–like longhouse. "A lot of the clearing was already done

 Eric and Laura's sons enjoy reading on the docklike entrance path beyond the flanking birch trees near the middle of the south face of their home.

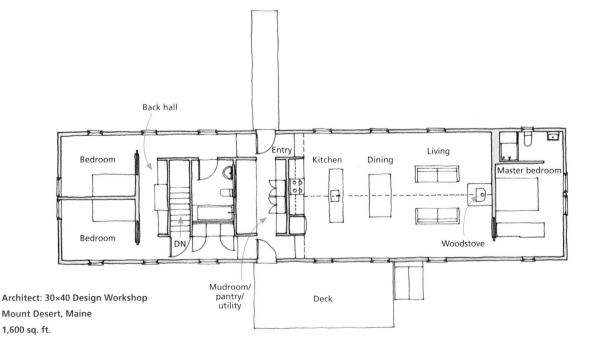

Architect: 30×40 Design Workshop
Mount Desert, Maine
1,600 sq. ft.

 Having the communal space toward the center of the longhouse mitigates the impression of the house's overall length; walls and doors on both ends stop your eye from perceiving the entire space at once, which lends the small house some mystery.

for us," he notes. Oriented east–west, his house overlooks grade that drops away from the long northern face toward the forest beyond, while the long southern face is washed with daylight most of the day and greets those arriving.

When asked if he had considered adding an ell to the plan or a second story, Eric responds quite practically that an ell would have been fighting the grade and that he didn't want to be climbing a lot of stairs. Also, "There's no view reason for going up," he explains. "I really wanted to have a pretty large open space. That seemed easier to build if we were just using a single level."

At 20 ft. by 80 ft., the considerable length of the small house makes a big statement from the exterior. It's organized around a central open kitchen/dining/living area anchored by a woodstove under a cathedral ceiling on scissor trusses. Flat ceilings on attic trusses cover both ends of the house, which accommodate private spaces: the master bedroom on the

A COMMUNAL SPACE

Anchored by the open kitchen on the east end and a woodstove on the west end (far right in photo above) with dining and living areas in between, the central communal space enjoys a generous gable cathedral ceiling and daylight from both sides. Chalkboard paint on the low wall that conceals kitchen counter clutter makes a great surface for the family to decorate for special occasions. Eric's drafting table quietly occupies a corner of the shared living area where he works when he isn't playing his guitar, in the foreground, with eight year-old Sig on the bass guitar. Ten year-old

Henning keeps his drums in his room.

A pantry behind the kitchen, in the multi-purpose mudroom, allows the open shelves in the kitchen to be sparsely populated, which helps keep the communal space from feeling cluttered. Low book-shelves in the communal space also provide storage without dominating the walls they abut. More storage shelves are tucked into the hall behind the shared bathroom and in the back hall outside the kids' rooms. It's much easier to keep everything in a small-house communal space in its place, if there's a place planned for everything.

 An efficient open-ended galley kitchen features IKEA cabinets with birch butcher-block countertops and IKEA open shelves. As part of the central service core, the kitchen and interior hall walls are painted a slight gray green, which differentiates them from the creamy white on the walls elsewhere.

 A deck just deep enough to accommodate a picnic table and circulation path, before the grade starts to slope off to the north, expands family living toward the peaceful view of the woods.

 The mudroom features a straight shot from the entry out the back door to the deck. Coir mats provide a durable nonslip walking surface, and the same limestone used in the shared bathroom offers an easily maintained surface to receive shoes and wet boots.

 The back hall outside the kids' rooms is very much connected to the perimeter circulation path around the core, but it also offers storage for games and a pocket for privacy where the boys can work on the computer or crafts at the desk. Since Eric and the boys have a fondness for trains and model trains, Eric enlarged an image of an old freight train that carried molten sulfur and printed it on Mylar® in a triptych.

western end and two smaller kids' bedrooms on the eastern end. Though he could have bundled all of the private spaces on one end and the communal spaces on the other, Eric saw the advantages of greater privacy for those in bedrooms on either end of the house. And since site constraints meant the driveway would be depositing folks to roughly the middle of the buildable area, it made sense to make the middle of the building the more public communal space.

Eric decided to float a core service area between the open family area and the kids' rooms. This more solid transitional zone serves as entry/mudroom/pantry/utility area and includes a shared bathroom, basement stairs, and kids' zone and offers multiple pockets for privacy. Circulation rings it. "To put the hallway to the outside, it can act as a gallery for us to hang artwork. It can collect light and bounce it around to the bedrooms, and it keeps all of those core spaces private and internal," says Eric. Plus, the boys enjoy racing around the perimeter and cutting through the entry/mudroom/pantry/utility area.

Large double-hung windows march in alignment down the north and south walls of the communal kitchen/dining/living area. It's more typical to treat windows on the north face of a house differently from those on the south. But Eric explains, "We wanted to be able to capture light on both sides equally." Also, he wanted to maximize forest views to

 Light gray Spanish limestone on the floor and shower walls of the shared bath are a splurge enabled by Eric's other budget choices. IKEA frosted cabinet door fronts act as a transom window above the tub/shower and allow the interior bathroom to borrow light from a window off the adjacent hall.

 In the master bedroom, a freestanding IKEA wardrobe that Eric customized with a sanded plexiglass back serves as both practical storage and a privacy wall, so Eric and Laura feel more removed from the adjacent communal space. Because the wardrobe doesn't extend to the ceiling and is partially translucent, the room feels larger than if a closet were built in.

Picking up on the geometry of the longhouse, parallel raised vegetable beds and a pea-stone path are centered on the paired large double-hung windows in the master bedroom at the end of the simple gable.

 The generous 3-ft. by 5-ft. windows have sills only 17 in. above the floor, which increases the connection to the outdoors that people in the kitchen work area or passing by feel, allowing the small house to live larger. Because finish carpentry is expensive and Eric has a taste for minimalist design, he chose not to include interior window, baseboard, or ceiling trim throughout the house.

the north, which smaller windows would have diminished. Because the large windows align, they lend the public space a sense of expansion to the outdoors in both directions, bringing the outdoors in. And folks working in the kitchen, seated at the dining table, or lounging by the woodstove can all take advantage of borrowed daylight and views across and through the open space.

Eric's longhouse is a new, small-house interpretation of the Native American and European versions from which he drew inspiration. He captures within a simple, economical form an expansive communal living space with ample access to daylight, ventilation, and views as well as pockets for privacy and more removed private quarters. His small longhouse makes a big statement about fresh versatility and simplicity.

PREFAB GLASS HOUSE

| SITE | 3D | DAYLIGHT | BIG/SMALL | MULTI-PURPOSE | PRIVACY | IN/OUT | FINISH PALETTE | QUALITY MATERIALS |

I GREW UP not far from architect Philip Johnson's late-1940s Glass House in New Canaan, Conn. We couldn't see the house from the road, but we understood from its mystique, even 25 years after it was constructed, that a glass house was state-of-the-art and something that few outside Johnson's rarefied circle would likely inhabit let alone experience. I never imagined that today, thanks to Taalman Koch Architecture's IT HOUSE building system, a prefab kit would be readily available, enabling folks to erect customized small glass houses of their very own, as lighting designer Terry Ohm has done in the Mayacamas Mountains of California.

> My comfort level is having less and having a very clean palette.

 Extra-wide ipé steps make a big statement and float on light-gauge, galvanized-steel stringers. Simple galvanized-steel posts and concrete piers touch lightly on the site, and, in a few locations, matching nonstructural galvanized-steel posts conceal utilities traveling up into the house.

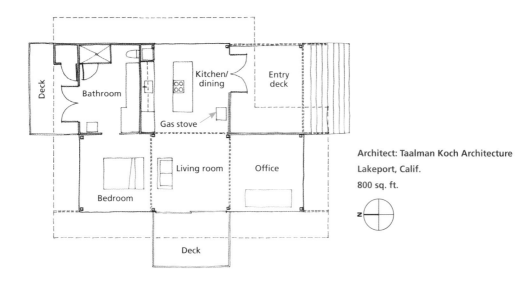

Architect: Taalman Koch Architecture

Lakeport, Calif.

800 sq. ft.

 Terry stands on the master-bath deck, one of three decks that expand living space and pockets for privacy beyond his glass house and out above the rural site.

Large expanses of glass allow a view from the entry deck clear through Terry's desk space to the trees beyond. Galvanized-steel ceiling panels extend from the inside out, as does aluminum framing.

"Living in a glass house you kind of feel like you're one with the outdoors, whether during the day when you can see the trees or at night when you can see the stars," says Terry, whose house is fairly remote and 3,000 ft. above sea level. It was important to Terry to disturb the site as little as possible, so he and his architects, Linda Taalman and Alan Koch, customized his house by raising it 4 ft. above grade (at its lowest point) and supported it on site-sensitive discreet piers. This meant they wouldn't need a lot of heavy equipment digging and pouring substantial concrete foundations. "I like being elevated. You have the wind and the air moving around the entire house, including below the house. . . . It makes it a

little more critter friendly as well; you're not as likely to find a rattlesnake in your house," notes Terry. Paying attention to the third dimension by elevating the house also enhances views from within it and on the decks.

When Terry first found the Taalman Koch IT HOUSE online, the architects offered two plan types to use as design starting points: a 1,200-sq.-ft. version and a 1,600-sq.-ft version. But Terry wanted a smaller house, so he and the architects developed an 800-sq.-ft. option. "I never felt like having a big house is necessary. So much of it doesn't get used. If you have a big house, you have to buy extra stuff to put in it," says Terry, who also appreciated that a smaller house would

 The multipurpose office/living/bed area opens into the kitchen to take best advantage of the small footprint. Daylight and views are borrowed across adjacent open spaces via floor-to-ceiling glass. Floors, built-in cabinets, and custom furnishings made of Monterey cypress add warmth to the aluminum, galvanized steel, and glass finish palette.

The Monterey cypress–clad kitchen shares the view with the rest of the house and includes a Squak Mountain Stone™ recycled-material countertop where Terry dines.

In Terry's office area, custom Monterey cypress bookshelves contain his edited collection of prized books. The full-height and partial-height glass walls practically dissolve away where they meet at the corner, making it seem as if the path leading up the slope comes inside and as if the house extends to the outside.

better accommodate his budget. These days, Taalman Koch Architecture offers Terry's plan as well as many other sizes as design starting points.

The T-shaped open kitchen/dining, living, bedroom, and office plan in combination with 450 sq. ft. of decks that provide pockets for privacy allow Terry's small house to live large. With no space wasted in halls and only one interior door leading to the bathroom/laundry area/closet, each multipurpose space borrows daylight and view from the other. Clad, for the most part, in floor-to-ceiling windows, the vast expanses of glass make a big statement inside and out, as do the extra-wide ipé stairs that seemingly float up from the rugged terrain to the entry deck.

The prefab kit—including precut and predrilled metal framing, hardware, glass, and finish materials to form the

full house—was flat-packed and shipped to Terry's mountain location to be clipped, bolted, and cabled together on site by a crew of two contractors. This process produces less on-site waste. "Having everything show up that's intentional for building that structure seems like a more practical way to build," remarks Terry, who also appreciates the quality of the materials used in the IT HOUSE. "To me, it has a nice balance between being really warm and also having that industrial edge to it," he notes. All of the interior wood is Monterey cypress milled from salvaged felled trees sourced by Evan Shively's Arborica, in northern California.

Full-height gray silk drapes (with a backing), which play off the house's many silver metal finishes, help soften the interior. Since the house doesn't have air-conditioning, Terry relies on cross breezes and the drapes to control daylight

WHAT IS IT?

Architects Linda Taalman and Alan Koch developed the IT HOUSE building system to do two things: to expand the indoor–outdoor lifestyle by reinventing the glass house and to push building technology and sustainability in what (at least in the United States) is considered a new direction. The architects named the system the IT HOUSE not for information technology but because *it* is a very open term and can be anything you want. The IT HOUSE is fabricated offsite and assembled onsite.

The highly customizable system typically includes precut and predrilled aluminum wall framing; steel deck roof; aluminum-framed double-glazed windows and doors by Metal Window Corporation; wall panels of fiber cement, 3form resin, and/or wood; galvanized-steel ceiling panels (inside and out); built-in cabinetry; and the hardware required to assemble the elements into a house. The materials are durable, generally recyclable, low maintenance, high quality, and shipped in small packages directly from the manufacturers. In Terry's case, the architects partnered with Blue Sky Building Systems, who provided the elevated light-gauge galvanized steel floor framing.

Once delivered, the components are erected in the field, often with the aid of someone the architects send to train local contractors in the assembly process. Local concrete installers, electricians, plumbers, and other subcontractors provide their services to render the IT HOUSE complete. "It works for local building departments, local jurisdictions; it works on sites where you don't want to bring in heavy equipment. The parts are small, and it just makes for a smarter construction process," says Linda.

 Open shelves in the kitchen lend variety to the otherwise flush built-ins and offer versatile easy access to everyday dishware. As part of his lighting design, Terry selected LED strip lights mounted to the rear of the open shelves to generate a warm soft glow.

The only interior passage door in Terry's house is this aluminum slider that leads to his sizable bathroom where he keeps his stacked laundry machines and clothes. The panels to the left are cement fiberboard and are used inside and out.

and solar heat gain, as well as a ceiling fan in his office space. Tapered rigid insulation on the roof, rigid insulation in the floor structure, and foil-faced rigid insulation in the non-glass walls also help mitigate the temperature. A propane-fueled gas heating stove in the kitchen area warms most of the house on colder mountaintop days, and solar panels remotely located behind the mechanical shed off the driveway generate electricity. Propane is also used to heat Terry's water and fuels his dryer, stove, and oven.

Terry's minimalist aesthetic works well for a glass house. He has pared down his belongings to those things that are most important to him. "I think the average person finds comfort in having lots of stuff, because most people do. . . . I'm kind of the opposite. My comfort level is having less and having a very clean palette," he explains. If you share Terry's sensibility, a small glass house might be right for you, too. Nowadays, you don't need to be Philip Johnson.

 The shower enclosure is, naturally, also glass. The interior shower walls are Caesarstone®, and the Starck shower pan is made by Duravit. A tall radiator appears somewhat sculptural on the back wall and is the only heat source, supplementing the gas stove.

THE 20K HOUSE

| SITE | 3D | DAYLIGHT | BIG/SMALL | MULTI-PURPOSE | PRIVACY | IN/OUT | FINISH PALETTE | QUALITY MATERIALS |

"WE BUILD A HOUSE; we watch how they live in it, and then the next year we try to do one better," says Andrew Freear, the director of the Rural Studio at the School of Architecture, Planning and Landscape Architecture at Auburn University in Alabama. The student-designed small, affordable model houses (known as 20K Houses) evolve from year to year and explore many of the same small-house design strategies seen in more expensive custom small houses. Each 20K House is donated to a member of the Hale County community.

Dave's House, which was the eighth 20K House built, evolved in response to the design of Frank's House, which was the second 20K House and is an interpretation of the shotgun style. Typically narrow and long with few windows on the side,

The 20K House is a house for everyone.

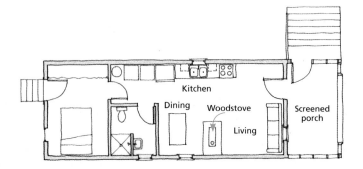

Dave's house (pp. 97–99)
504 sq. ft. plus porches

Designer: Auburn University Rural Studio Outreach Program
Hale County, Ala.

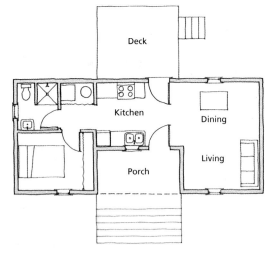

Mac's house (pp. 100–101)
504 sq. ft. plus porches

Joanne's house (pp. 102–103)
523 sq. ft. plus porches

 A full-width screen porch at the gable entry end of Dave's House makes a big statement on a small house. Like most of the 20K Houses, the house floats above the landscape on an efficient and economic girder system with concrete piers supporting girders that cantilever a short distance beyond the piers in opposite directions.

the shotgun-style house accommodates rooms or spaces that run front to back without a separate hallway. It can make for a very efficient and practical house. In the case of Frank's house, it's a mostly open multipurpose space with substantial porches on either end. But the students found that Frank didn't really know what to do with the two porches. So in Dave's House, they proposed one large inhabitable screened porch that spans the front instead, making a big statement on a small house. "You enter at the side, and then the front door is very close to the screened porch door, simply so the screened porch itself doesn't become a corridor. So you can use it as a room," explains Andrew. It receives daylight and breezes from three sides, and is both outdoors and indoors at once; you can also use it as a pocket for privacy off the primary living space.

Inside, the day space of the multipurpose sitting and dining areas features a woodstove on one side and the kitchen area running along the other. As you continue toward the rear of the house, you come upon the bathroom and the night space of the bedroom, which runs the full width of the house and includes an exterior door to a modest rear stoop.

To make the small house feel bigger, the ceiling in Dave's House is a generous 10 ft. high. Such attention to the third

THE RURAL STUDIO OUTREACH PROGRAM

Called the 20K House Project, the program aims for the model houses it creates to be constructed for $20,000, which the Rural Studio assumes to be the approximate loan amount someone in Hale County receiving median Social Security checks might be able to afford. Of the $20,000 budget, $13,000 is allocated to materials and $7,000 to labor and profit. At that price, the 20K House is intended to be a well-designed and well-built alternative to a trailer home that can be built in 3 to 4 weeks.

Recipients of the 20K House Project houses are required to own land (with private or public water and wastewater systems as well as other utility services) to accommodate the house and to provide the appliances. In order to create a small model house that may be suited to a variety of occupants, the students don't initially design with a specific client in mind and learn only later in the process where and for whom they will be constructing a 20K House. In the 10 years since Andrew Freear conceived of the 20K House Project, the Rural Studio Outreach program, generally composed of two to five postgraduate students per academic year, has built an impressive body of evolving work.

The porch ceiling at Dave's House extends all the way up to the underside of the roofing, creating an airy effect. White pine siding on the front enclosing wall provides a quality tactile surface that can be further personalized with paint or stain.

 Frank's House was one of the first 20K Houses built. Its shotgun style influenced the design of Dave's House. Some of the 20K Houses that were constructed after Frank's use painted siding, which seems less agrarian and more residential.

The open plan of Dave's House accommodates overlapping space for a variety of activities: sitting, dining, and cooking. The central location of the woodstove, complete with a brick hearth and rear wall, effectively heats the space while also providing a central gathering space and an accent feature.

 Mac sits on the porch of his modified dogtrot-style house. Natural pine wood trim and skirt boards, which conceal some of the pipes and wires under the house and help bring it closer to grade, add visual warmth. A nearby trailer contrasts the more permanent and more spacious 20K House.

dimension keeps Dave and his visitors cooler since there's room for hot air to rise above them. Ceiling fans throughout the house and on the porch also help with cooling. "If you go into a trailer home where a ceiling is 8 ft. or 7 ft. 6 in., they feel like the sardine cans that they are," notes Andrew. But the higher ceiling at Dave's House lends it a feeling of spatial generosity.

Mac's House came next and is a response to Dave's House. Rather than enter at the end of the open living space, as at Dave's House, a recessed porch along the side toward the middle serves as an entry and a pocket for privacy. A galley kitchen adjacent to the porch separates the open day space on one side from the night space on the other. Though the 504-sq.-ft. interior is the same size as Dave's House, and the overall form is similar, it is apportioned differently.

"What we like about Mac's is the two doors opposite each other," says Andrew. The front door in the recessed porch directly aligns with the back door, which opens onto a rear deck and offers additional opportunity to extend informal living outdoors. When both doors are open, the house is ventilated through the recessed porch, kitchen, and rear deck much like through the breezeway in a dogtrot-style house. Mac's modified dogtrot differentiates the interior spaces more than Dave's.

Finally, Joanne's House builds on the lessons of both Dave and Mac's House. Her house has the same perimeter length as Dave's but has a square plan unlike the narrower rectangular plans of Dave's and Mac's. In addition, her house is slightly larger at 523 sq. ft. of interior space. Joanne's porch occupies a partially recessed corner that invites daylight and breezes from two directions. A portion of it projects beyond the roofline to capture unfettered daylight and to reach out toward passersby and visitors. It serves the multiple purposes of entry, a meet-and-greet space, an outdoor living area, and a pocket for privacy. The porches on all three of the houses shown here significantly expand living space beyond the small-house walls.

 Mac stands between the front and the rear doors, which, when both open, ventilate the house as if through a breezeway. The galley kitchen opens onto the dining/living space, which has a generous 9-ft.-tall ceiling that helps the space feel more expansive (and cooler).

 Sealed natural pine trim, gray plywood floors, and white walls and ceilings throughout Mac's House help unify the interior so it is perceived as one continuous larger space rather than smaller broken-up spaces.

 The mostly recessed corner porch on Joanne's square house also reaches beyond the overhanging roof to grab some direct sun. The wall surfaces edging the porch, with which Joanne is in closest contact, are white-washed pine.

Joanne's kitchen, while open to the living/dining space, is distinct from it and edged with bookcases that add function while screening the kitchen prep area. Access to the glazed entry door and windows allow the open spaces to borrow daylight and view from each other. Tall windows in the 9-ft. walls reduce the amount of wall between the window heads and ceiling to better reflect light off the ceiling back into the interior.

The pressure-treated pine horizontal guard rail on Joanne's porch is solid to block the view into the house from those approaching the front door. It's slatted elsewhere so as to feel less enclosing and to extend living space farther into the landscape. Rafter tails are exposed at the eaves, but to avoid creating a dark space overhead, the rest of the porch ceiling is flat, rather than cathedral, and made from white beaded-board.

As in Mac's House, interior spaces are more clearly delineated in Joanne's House than in Dave's. A galley kitchen adjacent to the entry porch has views to the porch and out the front across the landscape and is somewhat removed from the living space, though still open to it. Andrew believes, "It's nice to be able to separate the kitchen space off a little bit. . . . I think it's good to contain the detritus of a kitchen in a kitchen, frankly." The design implications of the appliance locations are also carefully considered. "We have three-hour conversations at the Rural Studio about where to put the great ugly American refrigerator," notes Andrew. In Joanne's House it's in the corner close to a window where it might bounce outdoor light into the interior.

The entry door is centrally located, as with Mac's house, and provides easy access to day spaces on one side of the house and night spaces on the other. And like Dave's and

Mac's Houses, there aren't hallways at Joanne's that would waste space. To adhere to the tight budget, the exterior and interior finish palettes at each 20K House are fairly modest and succinct. The impact on the design and bottom line of every material variation is very carefully considered.

To make the 20K Houses accessible to a larger audience, the Rural Studio expects to make construction drawings of Dave's, Mac's, and Joanne's one-bedroom houses, as well as some two- and three-bedroom houses, available to the public. "The 20K House is a house for everyone, and we want folks to have access to it," says Natalie Butts, the communication and 20K House manager at the Rural Studio. "They would be a great mother-in-law cottage; they would be a really fantastic second home on a lake, your first home, or retirement home; it's for everybody."

WHITE ON WHITE

SITE | 3D | DAYLIGHT | MULTI-PURPOSE | PRIVACY | IN/OUT | FINISH PALETTE | QUALITY MATERIALS | DETAILS

THIS SMALL-HOUSE renovation by Priestley + Associates Architecture in Rockport Village, Maine, infuses a traditional New England form with a pared-down modern sensibility. Once a blacksmith shop, the now predominantly white exterior and interior display a combination of distinctive details integrated with a succinct finish palette. "Keeping the aesthetic very clean and very minimal has a calming effect," says architect John Priestley.

The house is pretty close to perfect the way that it is.

 Groupings of tall windows and a glazed side door face south and the view. A succinct palette of white painted shingles, minimal white trim and windows, a gray asphalt-shingle roof, ipé decks, and metal cable rails helps unify the form of the small house.

The renovation maintained the gable form of the one-time blacksmith's shop, updating it with knife-edge eaves and augmenting it with a shed dormer and a second-story cross gable on the west end. The one-story structure to the right encloses a lap pool, which is open to the sky.

Architect: Priestley + Associates Architecture
Rockport Village, Maine
1,360 sq. ft.

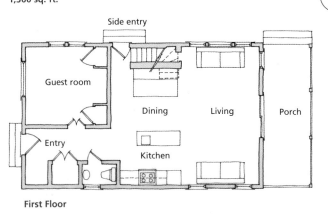

First Floor

Side entry

Guest room

Dining · Living · Porch

Entry

Kitchen

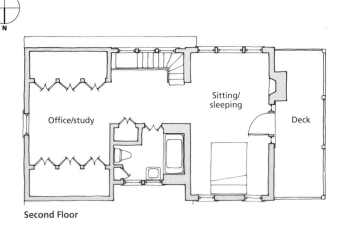

Second Floor

Office/study

Sitting/sleeping

Deck

N

Large rough-hewn granite steps and pea stone provide an interesting contrast to the crisp white, glazed side door, white shingle courses, and ipé board-walk path.

 The built-in dining bench is doubly efficient because the lid lifts off to reveal storage space inside. The glass table picks up on the light and airy theme of the space and efficiently accommodates six diners

 Cloaked with the same white tongue-and-groove boards as the walls and ceilings, the kitchen and its cabinets blend effortlessly into the open space. The beamed ceiling beyond is composed of the original floor joists wrapped in white boards, which gives the impression of a taller and more dynamic ceiling over the gathering areas than a continuous flat ceiling would.

Horizontal courses of white, painted shingles on the house exterior are echoed by white, horizontal courses of Azek®—joined with intentional reveals—that enclose an adjacent lap pool. Minimal white exterior trim on the house edges the roof rake and wall openings, calling little attention to itself. On the house interior, white tongue-and-groove boards are held a prescribed dimension apart (like the Azek wrapping the pool enclosure) to create a distinctive detail of repeated gaps that march around the walls and across the ceilings on both floor levels; interior trim is completely omitted.

The succinct palette of white, rhythmic tongue-and-groove boards allows the open sitting areas, dining area, and kitchen, which includes cabinets faced in the same boards, to blur into each other. The white board backdrop carries up the stairs and across the second-floor walls and ceilings, uniting the small house's varied open spaces into what feels like a generous nuanced space. A quiet, quartersawn, white oak floor runs throughout. Homeowners Michael Hampton and David Kantor were attracted to the crisp and airy effect. "I think we both were drawn to the simplicity of it, the views and the quality of light in the house," says Michael. Of course, they were also drawn to the location near the water in a village not far from Camden, Maine.

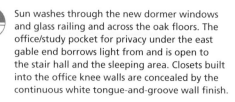

Sun washes through the new dormer windows and glass railing and across the oak floors. The office/study pocket for privacy under the east gable end borrows light from and is open to the stair hall and the sleeping area. Closets built into the office knee walls are concealed by the continuous white tongue-and-groove wall finish.

John designed the renovation for a previous owner who lived by herself. She and John adhered to the former blacksmith shop's footprint, which is in the local shoreland zone. Instead of expanding living space out, they increased the volume with a new dormer over a new stair and a new second-floor cross gable on the west end. John's original client envisioned an unconventional multipurpose second-floor living space open to her sleeping area and, on the first floor, an open kitchen off a roomy dining space looking out to the view. "Because it is a small house, any individual spaces would have seemed like closets, so the only separate space is a combination office/guest room on the first floor. Of course, there is a bathroom upstairs, but other than that, it is open, because otherwise I think it would be very claustrophobic," says John.

The upstairs sitting space off the sleeping area looks out to the Goose River and Rockport Harbor beyond, and borrows additional daylight from the stair hall. A deck to the right extends living space out toward the view. Custom chairs and ottomans designed by Michael and a small built-in wood-burning fireplace make it cozy.

The bed is located on the north end of the new second-floor cross gable where it's open to the sitting space overlooking the view. The carefully placed seams on the trim-free, tongue-and-groove wall and ceiling treatment are on full display.

Michael, an interior designer, and David had a different idea about how to use the spaces. It's a testament to the versatility of the multipurpose solutions created by John and the previous homeowner that Michael and David could swap the use of some of the spaces with great success. "On the first floor, we really wanted to utilize the small spaces as much as possible, while making it very comfortable," says Michael. While the previous homeowner had a substantial dining table

in the west end of the house toward the water view, Michael and David chose to locate two sitting areas there: a sofa and chairs grouping to the north, and a daybed area to the south. The daybed Michael selected is low so as not to hinder the view of Goose River through the sizable gang of three windows to the south that bring the outdoors in. Michael and David prefer having the living area on the more public first floor, rather than on the second floor where the previous homeowner placed it. Michael situated the dining area immediately adjacent to the stairs and near the kitchen island. "To best utilize that space, I designed a small upholstered bench, rather than have a set of chairs go all of the way around a dining table," explains Michael.

On the second floor, he and David located the office/study on the east end where the previous homeowner had positioned her bed. She had liked the idea of being able to lie in bed and look across the stair hall to the wood-burning fireplace on the west end of the second floor. Instead, Michael and David enjoy the pocket for privacy that the office/study provides off the stair hall, which is open to the sitting/sleeping area. "Generally, during the day, one of us is working in the office. And the nice thing about having that space is that the other one of us, whoever's not using the desk and the computer, is probably sitting at the other end of the bedroom in those comfortable chairs . . . , so we can still be occupying the same space, but we're not on top of each other," says David.

Michael and David plan to replace the lap pool and its enclosure with a one-car garage designed by John. It will occupy the footprint of the lap pool enclosure and have a one-story flat roof. "We told John, we love the purity of the form of the house as it is now, and we don't want an addition to take away from that," says Michael. "The house is pretty close to perfect the way that it is," notes David.

 Minimal cable rails on the second-floor deck off the sleeping/sitting area provide little distraction from the view beyond, which can be enjoyed from comfortable Adirondack chairs.

 The master bath vanity and tub feature natural finish accents of walnut, while the pattern of seams continues across the tongue-and-groove walls and is scored into the Corian® shower surround.

THE WEST WING

SITE 3D DAYLIGHT BIG/ SMALL MULTI- PURPOSE PRIVACY IN/OUT QUALITY MATERIALS

We loved our house; we didn't want to move.

ONE OF THE FIRST photos I ever saw of my sister- and brother-in-law's newly acquired property in Corte Madera, Calif., was of my mild-mannered brother-in-law, Doug, using a jackhammer in the backyard to break up asphalt on a sunny weekend. He and my sister-in-law, Alice, had been married about a year and were ready to put down roots in a great location near a bike path, park, and town in an early 1950s house that needed some T.L.C. inside and out. Apparently, on the West Coast, where much of life takes place outdoors, you often start a renovation by addressing the grounds. The Moores' rear yard and its relationship to

The ell of the master-suite addition bounds an outdoor room for grilling, dining, and entertaining

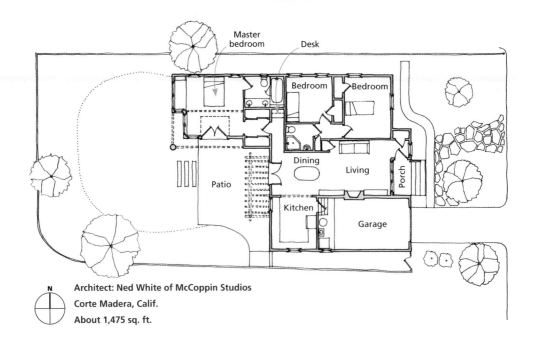

Master bedroom

Desk

Bedroom

Bedroom

Patio

Dining

Living

Porch

Kitchen

Garage

N

Architect: Ned White of McCoppin Studios

Corte Madera, Calif.

About 1,475 sq. ft.

Located close to the street, the front of the 1950s house has a quiet presence. Plantings partially shield the garage from view.

their house would be critical in creating bonus site-sensitive outdoor living and play space that would allow their modest house to live larger inside and out.

Next, Alice and Doug put in French doors so they could view their newly asphalt-free rear yard while welcoming western daylight into the dining area. Then they turned their attention to opening up the adjacent kitchen to the freshly sunlit dining area to create a multipurpose space. Fast-forward a few years and two kids later, and the two-bedroom, one-bathroom house was beginning to feel a bit cramped. They debated whether they should buy a bigger house, and, ultimately, decided to renovate and build an addition instead. "It was the more affordable option, but also we loved our house; we didn't want to move," explains Alice.

A modest front porch with a cheery red bench and throw pillows provides sheltered space for kids to await a ride or for guests to convene.

The living/dining space includes built-in shelving that flanks a fireplace on the wall bordering the garage. A kitchen alcove in the south-west corner opens to the common room. The rear dining patio and yard are visible from the entrance.

 The interior dining/living space opens to expand living space to the outdoor patio room.

The ensuing renovation/addition resulted in a new master suite ell that stretches to the west and shapes a patio grilling/dining/entertaining space close in to the house, complete with a shading arbor of wisteria. Granite landscape steps draw family and visitors past the embrace of the ell and up onto a modest clearing edged by fencing, perfect for lawn games. Having relocated to the "West wing" (as Alice and Doug refer to their new spacious master suite), the existing two bedrooms could be reconfigured to better suit daughter Lucy and son Charlie, while the original bathroom could be reconfigured and updated, too. A new full bath and his and her closets, flanking the suite's entry hall, round out the master suite's amenities.

When siting the addition, architect Ned White of McCoppin Studios recognized the potential of pushing the north face of the ell in alignment with the existing north face of the house so as to maximize the outdoor space to the south and to form an outdoor room. He then placed a window seat in the northwest corner of the master bedroom and a closet in the southeast corner to anchor and edge the slightly recessed walls that house French doors and windows. The recessed walls shield the south-facing French doors and west-facing windows from the sun's harshest light, and their cedar cladding visually warms the exterior and adds some welcome contrast to the original house's white stucco exterior.

The addition's grandest gesture is the cathedral ceiling featuring an inverted shed dormer that welcomes southern light deep into the new bedroom and invites Alice and Doug to view stars in the night sky from the bed below. Alice notes, "It's one of my favorite places to be in the house, especially toward the end of the day. The afternoon light back there is so pretty."

The hall to the master suite provides a quiet space for a shared family desk.

The built-in window seat offers a comfy spot to play the guitar or read, and accommodates four generous drawers that Alice admits she has claimed for herself.

When Alice discovered that the new foundation wall was bumping slightly into the interior of the master bedroom wall, she suggested creating a windowsill-height wainscot to absorb the extra thickness. Inspired by an idea she saw in a magazine, she also recommended incorporating the headboard into the wainscot design. "It was truly a happy accident," she recalls.

Thanks to the addition and renovation, the Moores' house continues to comfortably accommodate their active family of four. Though, Alice remarks, "You have to be so vigilant about your stuff; you can't let stuff accumulate." Storage closets, built-in shelves and drawers, and an attached one-car garage help keep their small house uncluttered and inviting. Alice concludes, "I think it works well for us because we like to spend time together, the four of us."

 A custom fir vanity with a granite countertop and matching granite tub deck with a partial-width glass shower door provide for some luxury in the new master bathroom that features affordable subway wall tile in the shower.

 The warm cedar cladding of the recessed wall that accommodates the bedroom's large casement windows and French doors is echoed on the exterior of the bold inverted shed dormer. A fat, round, stucco column receives the corner load and recalls the original house's finish and color.

PUBLIC–PRIVATE SWAP

SITE   3D   DAYLIGHT   MULTI-PURPOSE   PRIVACY   IN/OUT   FINISH PALETTE   QUALITY MATERIALS

THE OPEN LIVING/DINING/KITCHEN concept is a staple multipurpose solution in small houses. It eliminates the need for redundant halls and circulation paths, so multiple functions can be accommodated in less space, and it allows areas that serve different purposes to benefit from borrowed daylight and views across spaces serving different needs. Deciding how to arrange and where to place an open communal space is fundamental to its success. On its most basic level, it can come down to where to place the open public space versus the private spaces of bedrooms and bathrooms.

The sizable east-facing window . . . has a front porch feel because we can see neighbors walking the dogs, driving by.

 The rear deck, now easily accessible from the open living/dining/kitchen space, expands living space outdoors along a 6-ft.-tall privacy fence made of the same treated pine decking that's under foot. Rusted steel tubes, which match those used to support the perforated steel panels along the bamboo garden, provide a destination for tea lights strung overhead.

Before

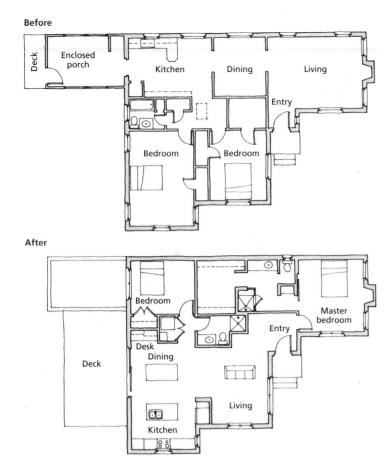

After

N
Architect: Allen Architecture
Fort Worth, Tex.
1,300 sq. ft.

Architect Brandon Allen and his then soon-to-be wife, Anissa, decided early on that they would need to flip the public and private spaces in their late-1940s fixer-upper to take best advantage of its footprint and site.

The house is located in an established neighborhood of mostly prewar houses, so Brandon and Anissa chose to leave the exterior form largely unchanged, in keeping with the scale, rhythm, and context of the neighborhood. This was also a cost-effective strategy. However, the existing interior layout would need to be completely revamped. "There was zero connection to the outside," Brandon notes. "We knew we wanted to open that up." The plan of the house when they acquired it had the public spaces of a separate living room, dining room, and kitchen lined up from front to back along the north face of the house, which borders the neighbors' driveway. These more public rooms ended in a dilapidated enclosed porch that Brandon and Anissa promptly had removed. The private spaces of two bedrooms and the house's only full bath were on the south staggered side of the house that faces the

Painting the exterior brick a midtone earthy gray and the entry and garage a slightly darker color in a related family sets the stage for the interior color palette and the homeowners' quietly modern aesthetic.

 The large eastern-facing window on the front of the house washes the open living/dining space with morning light and provides views of neighborhood activity. A smaller clerestory-like south-facing window admits light filtered through the adjacent magnolia and makes room for the TV.

The shared view to the backyard and access to warm western light from the open living/dining/kitchen space were critical to Brandon and Anissa's design.

 Brandon bumped the ceilings up 8 in. in areas over the kitchen/dining and living space to break up the ceiling plane and to provide more definition to those spaces. A solid-surface countertop on the island and a tile backsplash pick up on the faint earthy gray wall and ceiling color used throughout. Simple Shaker-style cabinets match the dark color of the entry feature and new garage outside.

 Just as Brandon found unique uses for steel outside his small house, he improvised a use for steel inside, too. The kitchen counter, which contains the cooktop, is ½-in. plate steel. Brandon spent the better part of a day buffing oil into the steel, alternating between tung oil and linseed oil. It later took four people to lift the steel into place

A desk tucked in off the open space provides a pocket for privacy and a place to collect and organize the ephemera of everyday life.

driveway. The master bedroom was approximately the size of the living room and abutted the prime real estate of the backyard.

After an initial walk-through of the house, Brandon and Anissa recognized that it would make more sense to locate the more public spaces on the staggered south wall toward their driveway and to open up those spaces so they could all benefit from view, daylight, and access to the backyard. It followed that moving the bedrooms to the north side and closing up most of the north-facing windows to preserve sound and visual privacy from the neighbors would also be wise. Swapping public and private spaces meant that the fireplace would be in the master bedroom rather than in the living

room, but in Texas this isn't a hardship. The climate just doesn't really call for it.

Brandon located a new west-facing 9-ft.-wide slider off the back of the now open living/dining/kitchen, which leads to a new deck and offers expansive views of an enormous oak tree in the backyard. The 6-ft. 8-in.-wide by 6-ft.-tall east-facing window opening, which had been smaller and bordered what was a closed-off front bedroom, now graces their living room. Thanks to the large east and west openings there's some transparency from front to back. Brandon remarks, "You get a nice view of the large oak in the rear as you approach the front door," which contributes to the house's open feel. The sizable east-facing window on the front of the house offers

 A custom oiled-pine barn slider fits flush in the wall of the master bedroom and adds interest whether open or closed. The warm wood complements the reclaimed white oak floor found throughout the small house.

another bonus. "It almost has a front porch feel because we can see neighbors walking the dogs, driving by; we can wave, actually, if I'm sitting on the couch," says Brandon. On the weekends, this is his favorite place to enjoy a cup of coffee and a magazine.

Naturally, flipping the public and private spaces in the house also influenced how Brandon and Anissa addressed the rest of their property. With the open living/dining/kitchen oriented toward the driveway and backyard, both those areas warranted their attention. "We treated the driveway . . . as an extension of the landscape," Brandon notes. As with the

interior, Brandon used a succinct finish palette in the land-scape. Concrete flatwork with 4-in. expansion joints steps toward the garage and borders steel-edged planters and planting areas. In the front, a long stretch of concrete reaches toward limestone entry steps, and on the rear, a narrow run of concrete abuts a flush steel plate that transitions between the concrete and limestone stepping-stones leading to the deck.

Bamboo had been encroaching upon the house when Brandon and Anissa acquired the property, so they cut it back to the face of the new garage, which sits on the footprint of the unsalvageable original garage. They liked the idea of bamboo as a privacy screen and as a backdrop for the view out the new glass sliders, but they wanted to delineate a boundary to contain it and edge an outdoor room off the deck. Brandon turned to perforated steel to provide that boundary. The rusty red steel nicely complements the green bamboo. "It really pops," says Brandon.

With a clear vision and crisp aesthetic, Brandon and Anissa shaped a more open, updated small house better connected to the outdoors and their neighborhood, which also comfortably accommodates what—with the arrival of their daughter, Lula, two years ago—has become a family of three, plus Camper, the dog.

The rusty steel perforated panels act as a scrim of sorts in the late afternoon and draw interest while bounding the bamboo garden.

 A giant oak tree provides a focal point for the outdoor room and seasonal shade for those on the deck. A steel plate paver transitions between concrete and limestone stepping-stones en route to the rusted perforated steel panels that slide past each other to create a passageway to the rear bamboo garden.

AN ARTIST'S HOUSE

| 3D | DAYLIGHT | BIG/ SMALL | MULTI- PURPOSE | PRIVACY | IN/OUT | FINISH PALETTE | QUALITY MATERIALS |

PAT WARWICK HAS lived in 18th-century houses for most of her adult life. When she came upon the comparatively young 1880–1881 Charles McCanna House in downtown Warren, R.I., she knew it had potential. At 1,200 sq. ft. with a south-facing private backyard and just steps from the harbor, shops, and restaurants, it satisfied all of her primary criteria. But it would need some work. "It was just awful," Pat notes. Okay, it would need a lot of work.

There's a nice ease between antique and modern.

 A ceramic fish wall mirror (made by Pat) reflects the stairs to the second floor off the entry, which Pat opened up. The pale cream color of the second-floor wall extends down the back of the stair hall and provides a pleasing backdrop to the light chartreuse wall color downstairs and the green-gray trim.

The side entry porch provides a buffer from the street.

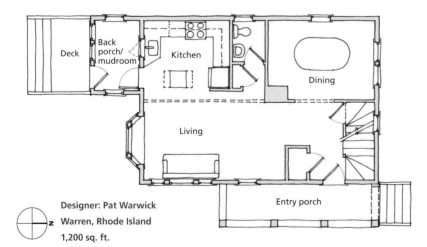

Designer: Pat Warwick
Warren, Rhode Island
1,200 sq. ft.

Deck

Back porch/mudroom

Kitchen

Dining

Living

Entry porch

Charles McCanna House
1880–81
WARREN PRESERVATION SOCIETY

According to the Warren Preservation Society, Pat's house belonged to Charles McCanna who worked in Warren at Cutler Mills, which manufactured textiles. Today, Pat's art studio is in the very same building.

 The open living space benefits from the new large bay window, which shares the proportions of the ganged double-hung windows in the east wall.

With an appreciation for Sarah Susanka's *The Not So Big House* book series, Pat focused her design savvy and artist's eye on the renovation. She and her builder came to believe that the house had been built out of parts over time; nothing seemed to match, not the windows or trim, and the stairs to the second floor seemed curiously wide for such a small house. Pat knew she would need to develop a succinct language of elements that would be readily visible throughout the soon to be less-chopped-up house. She discreetly opened up spaces to improve flow, increase access to daylight, and create a sense of spaciousness. "I like to keep the old but add some modern touches to it. I like to meld it somehow, so that there's a nice ease between antique and modern," says Pat.

Her instincts on the first floor were to remove enclosing walls and add a large bay window in the back south-facing wall that borders the living space. "The kitchen was like a black hole," she remembers. After removing the wall between it and the now brighter living space, she had a French door installed off the kitchen out to the reconfigured enclosed porch/mudroom, so the multipurpose spaces could share even

The boatlike kitchen features durable ipé counters and door frames on overhead glass cabinets for a fraction of the cost of teak. A movable island has a matching ipé top. Daylight streams through an interior window and French door that lead to the enclosed porch/mudroom.

ARTIST IN RESIDENCE

Pat took her time deciding which of her hand-crafted tile themes to install in her own custom shower. The blue crab and school of fish are perennial favorites among her customers, so, in the end, they were a natural choice.

With a degree in graphic design from the Rhode Island School of Design, experience working at the Woods Hole Oceanographic Institute as a designer and illustrator, and a childhood spent summering in the beach town of Old Lyme, Conn., Pat's transition to creating ceramic surfaces featuring aquatic and coastal habitat creatures was somewhat organic. Having come to the art form from a graphics background, "I was loving the colors and layers of color that I could get," she says. "With most ceramic artists, it's all about the clay; with me, it's all about the glazes," she clarifies.

Pat's ceramic surfaces are made of low-fire earthenware into which she either applies carved impressions (for her production line) or draws (for commissions) and then hand paints layers of commercial glazes. Samples of her work are sprinkled throughout her house, in the form of a hall mirror, kitchen wall hanging, trivets, coffee table, and, of course, in the shower tile installation.

The new, generous, stall shower that replaced the tub was the ideal place to install some of Pat's tile designs.

 Pat changed the roofline on the rear enclosed porch/mudroom and added the deck and full-width exterior stairs to graciously expand living space outdoors. Raised beds have accommodated vegetables, marigolds, and nasturtiums.

more daylight. She then fashioned an efficient kitchen influenced by her experience living on boats and cooking in their galleys for six years. To catch a glimpse outside while doing dishes, she had an interior window placed over the kitchen sink that opens to the enclosed porch/mudroom and borrows the view out to the backyard beyond. She appropriated space in the north end of what had been the original larger and less-efficient kitchen for a new half-bath and closet.

Because the view through the house to the north was also important to her, and she wanted the entry hall to feel more gracious, Pat had the wall that was enclosing the stairs to the second floor removed. She specified stair nosing and trim details as well as a balustrade that befit the house's vintage. Upstairs, she took a similar approach, removing walls,

creating alcoves, and installing skylights above to improve ventilation and brighten spaces.

Pat applied the same sense for clarity and depth of color seen in her ceramic surface designs to the color palette for the house. The trim throughout is a light green-gray that takes on different tones, depending on the available light and adjacent color. The first floor is a light chartreuse except for the dining room, which faces north, which she wanted to warm up with a berry color. The second floor is a custom pale cream color, and both bathrooms are soft lavender. The overall effect is succinct, light, and inviting. "After the renovation, I liked the airiness of it," concludes Pat.

Thanks to the half-wall guardrail, an alcove at the top of the stairs has breathing room and provides a cozy spot to sit and watch TV.

A new large skylight on the eastern side of the bedroom draws you toward it and past the master bath to your right.

"I'm not a big curtain person," says Pat. The large frosted bathroom window stays closed and provides privacy. A small skylight above admits fresh air and direct sunlight.

TOWER HOUSE

SITE   3D   DAYLIGHT   BIG/SMALL   MULTI-PURPOSE   PRIVACY   IN/OUT   FINISH PALETTE   QUALITY MATERIALS   DETAILS

WHERE SPACE IS limited, you need to get creative. A smart example in this small house in Portland, Oreg., is the wall of nested cubbies that divides the living room and bathroom (as shown in the photo on the facing page). It's such a simple solution that you can't help but wonder why we don't see more examples of it. Rather than build shelves on either side of a wall to serve two rooms, which would result in a wall around 30 in. thick, Matt nested cubbies facing the living room and cubbies facing the

We're part of the neighborhood and part of nature.

The taut tower features large and narrow window groupings as well as a square window, which plays off the square face of the house. Matt says, "Both of us have very austere taste, so those types of compositions appeal to us."

 The double-sided nested cubbie wall serves the living space on one side and the bathroom on the other. The composition of solid and void is somewhat reminiscent of the composition of solid (siding) and void (windows) on the exterior of the house.

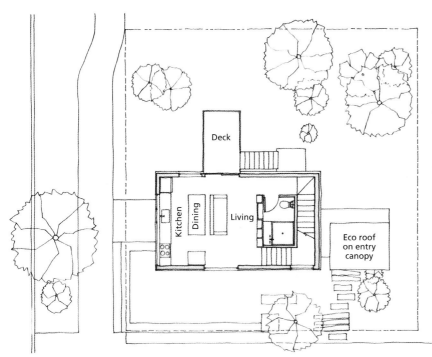

Architect: Matt Kirkpatrick at Design for Occupancy

Portland, Oreg.

704 sq. ft.

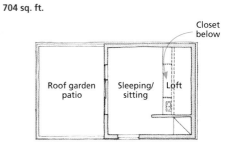

Forest Stewardship Council®-certified sapele veneer plywood faces custom kitchen cabinets, the dining table, side table, and coffee table. The warm reddish wood features a ribbon-like grain that Matt has oriented horizontally, which echoes the grain of the Glulam beams above, the kitchen window orientation, and the horizontal slatting of the exterior cedar. The color also complements the tiger wood floors.

bathroom into a single 12-in.-thick wall. What appears as a blank area on one side is actually cubbies on the other. It's a space-saving artful design that is born of practicality, much like the exterior of the home Matt Kirkpatrick designed for himself and his wife, Katherine Bovee, who have since been joined by their daughter, Amara.

Matt located and sized windows—some large and vertical, some skinny and horizontal—where light and views are paramount to the interior. Areas that appear blank on the exterior of their diminutive cedar-clad tower are deliberately functional, accommodating interior cabinetry, stairs, storage, and privacy. Areas enclosed with skipped slatted cedar up top

bound a roof garden patio. And, yes, their house is noticeably different from their neighbors'. With a footprint of only 16 ft. by 28 ft., it occupies roughly 20% of its 50-ft. by 50-ft. lot, which is half the size of the typical 50-ft. by 100-ft. lots that surround them. Matt and Katherine elected to build up rather than out to preserve green space. In addition, they incorporated green space into the house itself in the form of flat eco roofs on the entry canopy, the upper-level patio, and the very top of the building.

Fortunately, when Matt and Katherine were building the house, the city of Portland was offering incentives for storm-water management systems like eco roofs. "It was financially

WHY USE SIPS?

Structural insulated panels (SIPs) are high-performance assemblies composed of rigid insulation sandwiched between skins of structural sheathing. Most of the SIPs used for exterior walls on Matt and Katherine's house were designed to nest with nominal 2×6 stud walls; they're made of 5½ in. of expanded polystyrene (EPS) insulation with ½-in. oriented-strand board (OSB) on either side. The exterior wall at the stairs is a little thicker to account for its greater unsupported height. The SIPs used for the roof are 12 in. thick and are supported by exposed Glulam® beams that help carry the load of the eco roof.

Once delivered to a building site, SIPs can be erected fairly quickly. It took about a week to construct the SIPs used in Matt and Katherine's house. SIPs are more efficient (yielding R-26 walls in this house) than conventional framing, so the heating system can be smaller, which results in both cost and space savings. Matt and Katherine have 1,500-watt electric heaters on each floor and generally use only one. "It's basically like having a hair dryer in your wall," says Matt. The tighter envelope requires fresh air ventilation in the form of either a heat recovery ventilator or energy recovery ventilator. Matt and Katherine have the former in the basement. They don't have a central cooling system; they simply open their windows on cool evenings to bring down the temperature of the house.

The east-facing entry is sheltered by a planted roof canopy that brims with grapevines and is partially enclosed on the street-facing side with slats of cedar, creating a semiprivate porch-like space.

The long band of windows above the kitchen counter provides ongoing views of the streetscape. "I feel a real connection to the outside world. . . . We're part of the neighborhood and part of nature," says Katherine.

cost neutral, more or less, for us, and, of course, there were all sorts of other benefits for having a green roof, like we could have an outdoor patio up top, so it really created another room for us," notes Katherine. Matt adds, "Thermal mass on the roof helps modulate temperature," which fits in nicely with their goal to follow passive house principles, as did building with structural insulated panels (SIPs) and using triple-glazed windows and doors.

Built across three levels, the house functions more like three stacked, mostly open rooms. The unfinished basement level is one room. The main level includes the kitchen/dining/living area in one room, a deck, and a full bathroom. The upper level is made up of a sleeping/sitting area/closet in one room with a loft, and an outdoor room in the form of the roof garden, whose skipped slatted cedar walls offer privacy without completely obscuring the view. Matt incorporated generous ceiling heights to give each level some

Building small meant that Matt and Katherine could afford a few splurges in their budget, including this Japanese soaking tub. Because the tub is so large Matt and Katherine selected a gray-water toilet/sink combo for both its space-saving dual purpose and its water-saving efficiency. Water that you rinse your hands with fills the toilet tank.

 A library sliding ladder provides access to Matt and Katherine's sleeping loft. There's just enough room beneath for clothes hanging, storage, and a sink.

breathing space. The main level has a 10-ft.-high ceiling, and the upper level a 12-ft. ceiling, which made room for a loft above the stairs. Matt deepened the loft just enough to fit clothes-hanging space and a second sink below.

When Matt and Katherine first moved into their new house, there were just the two of them. The upper level acted as a master suite, with their bed below, a desk area up above in the pocket for privacy the loft offered, and a dining space out in the roof garden. Then came daughter Amara. Undaunted, they moved their sleeping space up to the loft and placed a baby futon down below for their daughter. These days, they find it easier to enjoy outdoor meals on the main-level deck, after sliding the table out the screen doors, than on the upper-level roof garden. They have plans for a 200-sq.-ft. addition to include two bedrooms and a bathroom above the entry patio, which will bring the living area to a grand total of around 900 sq. ft., not including the unfinished basement. Katherine says maybe in another decade they'll finish the basement because they equipped it with plumbing in the event they want a bathroom down there some day. That's the sum total of their expansion plans for the house.

"It feels really roomy. . . . It definitely exceeded my expectations and it lives really well," concludes Katherine. They rely on the many amenities Portland has to offer, like the nearby playground at the elementary school, Amara's day care two blocks away, and off-site working, dining, and entertainment venues to round out their needs. The house, in combination with neighborhood, handily serves them.

A narrow, vertical window in the stairway takes advantage of the tall space to frame a view of the neighbors' chimney. As a result, the stairway feels less confining (and more exhilarating).

 Matt and Katherine chose unfinished western red cedar rain-screen siding for its durability, for the way it reveals its age, and for what Matt describes as "a certain honesty of elements." At the upper patio level, it's attached to a steel frame and maintains the same ½-in. gaps as the siding below (for privacy) until it clears railing height and every other board is omitted to create a more porous enclosure.

The upper level has satisfied a variety of uses as the family has grown. It currently accommodates their music collection, Amara's sleeping and play space, and access to the roof garden patio which extends their living space. The roof is planted with licorice ferns, coastal strawberries, camass, various sedums, creeping thyme, nodding onions, big leaf lupine, and prickly pear cactus.

CALIFORNIA COMPOUND

| SITE | 3D | DAYLIGHT | MULTI-PURPOSE | PRIVACY | IN/OUT | FINISH PALETTE | QUALITY MATERIALS | DETAILS |

We really use every inch of the property.

JOSH HEISER AND Steve Burns found a nearly half-acre parcel in Sonoma, Calif., that had the basic ingredients they would need to shape a site-sensitive small-house compound. It was near downtown Sonoma Square, adjacent to a creek, and featured several small structures, including a 1880s cook shack. "We like to live small," notes Steve, so the opportunity to live among small buildings in a variety of outdoor living environments in a seasonable climate appealed to him and Josh.

The brick patio in front of the backhouse is furnished for both outdoor dining and lounging. Josh chose colors for the board-and-batten siding and windows that would slightly recede into the landscape. By contrast, the color of the new Dutch door, inspired by the antique gate, pops.

Josh designed a woven, rusted-steel front gate inspired by the woven redwood fence he designed on the side of the property. He calls it a "friendly neighbor fence" because it looks the same on both sides.

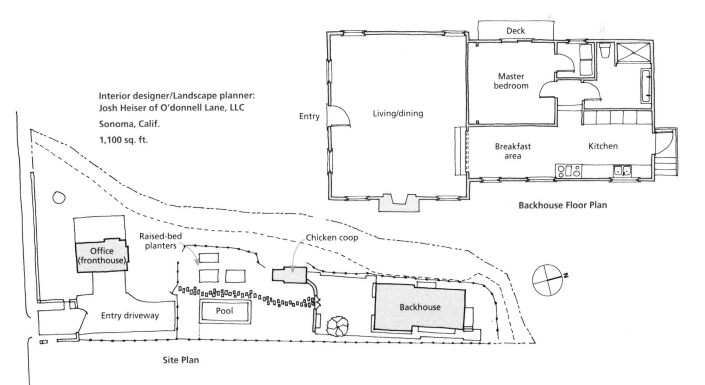

Interior designer/Landscape planner:
Josh Heiser of O'donnell Lane, LLC
Sonoma, Calif.
1,100 sq. ft.

Backhouse Floor Plan

Deck

Master bedroom

Entry

Living/dining

Breakfast area

Kitchen

Site Plan

Office (fronthouse)

Raised-bed planters

Chicken coop

Entry driveway

Pool

Backhouse

A limestone path meanders between the raised beds and modestly sized saltwater pool in one of the property's three primary outdoor rooms. The chicken coop lies ahead to the left. Josh and Steve have seven laying hens and use the eggs to barter with their neighbors for tomatoes, peaches, and biscotti.

Tucked among similar lot sizes fronting a fairly busy street, Josh and Steve devised a series of courts that become increasingly private as you travel deeper within the site away from the street toward the north. With the aid of fences, walls, gates, and plantings the broad strokes of three outdoor rooms extend living space into a variety of outdoor settings.

After you enter onto a brick driveway, you encounter a woven steel gate (designed by Josh) that leads to the front house, which was built in the 1950s as a music studio and is now used by the homeowners as their office. Next, you come to a redwood woven fence featuring another woven steel gate that leads to a court containing a narrow saltwater pool on one side and three raised-bed planters (with redwood woven

sides like the fence) along with a chicken coop on the other. This is a generous combination entertaining, swimming, and gardening space that also contains pockets for privacy. Continue farther and you come upon the fieldstone wall Josh and Steve had constructed as the next threshold. There, pass through an antique gate and enter the more private domain of what Josh and Steve call the "backhouse" and the brick patio they use for entertaining smaller groups of friends.

The backhouse, where Josh and Steve live, includes a front open living/dining area that was constructed on a slab in the 1950s. The rear section of the house dates back to a cook shack (built about 1880) that later contained two bedrooms, a shared bath, and the kitchen. It was on a tenuous wooden

 The shared cathedral ceiling, new walnut floors, and white and black palette help unite the open living/dining and kitchen beyond. Artwork by Scott Coppersmith in the shape of California (made of reclaimed lath that relates to the floor tone) is a striking accent on the back wall.

 Josh and Steve use the ladder hanging on the wall in the foreground to access the open shelves in the tall storage area. The door at the end of the efficient galley kitchen leads to the grill area.

Upholstered seating and cheerful repurposed wooden signs announcing ice cream flavors make for a cozy kitchen table for two.

foundation essentially at grade. Because the backhouse is within the setback for the creek, Josh and Steve's remodel needed to maintain the existing footprint. But the cook shack required a new foundation, so Josh and Steve raised the floor level in that area to accommodate it. Turns out the level change between the living/dining area and kitchen was fortuitous. "When we sit down for dinner, it's nice that you're not looking into the kitchen even though it's all open," says Josh. Paying further attention to the third dimension, Josh and Steve elected to raise the bedroom/bathroom floor level up from the kitchen level. "As with every party, everybody

stands in the kitchen . . . and it feels like the bedroom is its own little area because you have to go up two steps to get there," says Steve.

Josh and Steve opened the ceiling in the kitchen and the relocated bathroom (which occupies a former second bedroom) to capture as much space as possible in the third dimension. The new cathedral ceiling in the kitchen matches the cathedral ceiling in the living/dining area and helps better link the kitchen area to the lower living/dining area, while allowing them to borrow light and view. The increased ceiling height in the kitchen makes room for tall storage opposite

 A new shallow balcony-like deck off the master bedroom overlooking the creek below is another favorite pocket for privacy, which also happens to bring the indoors out. The closed interior door ahead leads to the laundry closet, which used to be the shared bath.

the kitchen work area. Because Josh is 6 ft. 1 in. and Steve is 6 ft. 4 in., they didn't want overhead cabinets to bump into, opting instead for open shelves above the full-depth storage cabinets, refrigerator, and freezer on the wall that borders the relocated bathroom.

Josh's redesign of the kitchen included placing a door at the far end to access a rear barbeque area where Steve likes to grill and where they can enjoy a quiet private sitting area in the shade. The change from the original U-shaped kitchen layout to a galley configuration significantly improved the flow. The length of the space allows room for a small table and two comfortable chairs where, when they're not entertaining or dining at the table on the level below, Josh and Steve enjoy most of their meals. The table's slightly elevated location on the edge of the open living/dining space makes it an ideal pocket for privacy to enjoy a cup of coffee or the morning paper.

Recognizing that the open kitchen and multipurpose dining/living area are visible all at once, Josh adhered to a simple color palette in the shared spaces. "The Apple White paint, for me, makes the spaces feel a little bigger. There's so much color and vibrancy on the outside of the house; I didn't want the two things to compete." In the remodeled bathroom, which is well removed from the shared kitchen and living/dining area, Josh was comfortable reintroducing some of the tones and materials visible on the site.

And it is the site and the landscape design that tie the various living spaces together. The backhouse is in many ways only one of many layered living areas on the property. It could even be considered a pocket for privacy. "The house is really the ultimate California house because of the indoor–outdoor living we can experience pretty much year round," notes Steve. "We really use every inch of the property," adds Josh.

Reclaimed boards from the ceiling of the cook shack serve as wall finish in the bathroom. The painted patina of the redwood boards complements the slate tile used for the shower and creates a warm welcoming personal retreat.

 Opening the ceiling in the remodeled bathroom makes room for an oversize antique English mirror, which lends the modest room a sense of spaciousness. Salvaged redwood chicken watering troughs are repurposed as open bins for bathroom toiletries. Staying on theme, the hexagonal pattern of the slate floor tile is reminiscent of chicken wire.

A NARROW HOUSE

SITE 3D DAYLIGHT BIG/SMALL MULTI-PURPOSE PRIVACY IN/OUT FINISH PALETTE QUALITY MATERIALS DETAILS

THE CHALLENGE WITH any row house is drawing daylight from either end into the center. The longer the house, the greater the challenge, and the narrower the house, the longer it can seem. Architects Jennifer Mowery Marsh and Brian Marsh understand this all too well. After living on two floors with two kids in their 1889 row house in Hoboken, N.J. (and renting out the first floor) for six years, they were ready to tackle the row-house challenge and renovate three floors to call their own. In addition, they aimed for their reimagined quarters to meet the passive house standard.

Because street context and continuity are important to Jen and Brian, they elected to retain the original front brick facade with one exception; they swapped the leaky double-hung vinyl replacement windows for energy-efficient Intus PVC triple-glazed windows that are in keeping with their passive house strategy. Like many of their neighbors, they took a more contemporary approach toward the more private rear facade. Two enormous

When you're limited to 13 ft. 6 in. wide . . . everything is all relative to that width.

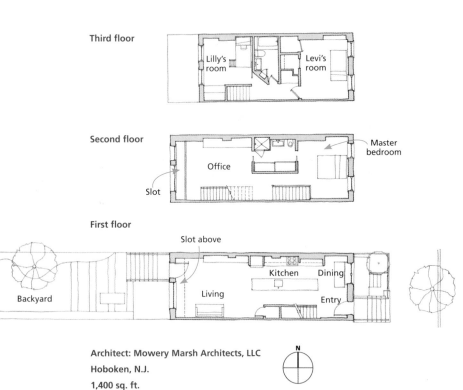

Third floor

Lilly's room | Levi's room

Second floor

Office | Master bedroom

Slot

First floor

Slot above

Backyard | Kitchen | Dining | Living | Entry

Architect: Mowery Marsh Architects, LLC
Hoboken, N.J.
1,400 sq. ft.

On the back of the house, a smaller venting window and operable door team with large fixed windows to form a tall rectangular assemblage that looks onto a small patio and AstroTurf® yard.

Based on the front of the row house, you might expect compartmentalized rooms and traditional moldings inside. But you would be in for a surprise.

 The open kitchen island unabashedly takes advantage of the row house's length to provide island seating toward the front of the house and sink work surface toward the living area.

In the living area, the large window brings the outdoors in and the narrow slot in the floor above provides visual access to the upper window, too. "I like having the muntins to break down the scale of the big window a little bit and not feel so modern," says Jen. Because the muntins are black, "You don't get the division as much, so it really does feel like full glass," she continues.

Jen and Brian decided to include their office among the house's more public spaces, so it's somewhat connected to the living room via the slot to the rear, the large window that spans the floor levels, and the semiopen stair to above. The result is an expansive environment for creative work.

6-ft.-wide, fixed, triple-glazed windows stack in the back, facing west. The lower window in the first-floor living room is 8 ft. 6 in. tall, and the window above it, off their office, is 10 ft. tall, which, in combination, make a big statement on a small house. Because they have two floors within that height, they held the second floor in their shared office back 3 ft. from the exterior wall, so daylight from the upper window could wash down into the first floor as well. The "slot" in the floor, as they call it, also contributes to a sense of openness.

Daylight streaming in the rear expanse of glass is visible across the open multipurpose plan from the front sunny dining alcove on the first floor and the front master bedroom on the second floor.

They chose to leave the rear wall on the third floor in its original location, which doesn't extend as far back as the first two floors. Jen and Brian see the top floor, where the kids' rooms are, as the most private. Smaller venting tilt-turn windows (also from Intus) work well on the front of son Levi's

Outfitted with a large table and built-in window seat, the dining niche accommodates all of the family meals and the occasional game night or client meeting.

room and the back of daughter Lilly's room. A skylight above the stairs brightens it and the kids' shared hall.

Fortunately, on all three floors light bounces well from side to side off the white brick party wall to the south and the white gypsum wall to the north. Fitting everything in within the narrow space is another matter. "When you're limited to 13 ft. 6 in. wide . . . everything is all relative to that width," says Jen. The first-floor circulation and kitchen area required that they pay attention to every inch. The kitchen island is 28 in. wide and one sided; the working aisle is 2 ft. 10 in. wide, and the walking isle is 3 ft. 2 in. wide. (The stair width was a given.) In suburban new construction such dimensions might seem insufficient, but Jen and Brian have found the tighter dimensions to be suitably sufficient for city living. The 14-ft. 6-in.-long kitchen island easily compensates for the lack of available width for a two-sided island.

WHAT MAKES IT PASSIVE?

Passive house retrofit/construction aims to reduce heating and cooling energy consumption by up to 90% from conventional retrofit/construction. Though not yet certified as a passive house, Jen and Brian's house was retrofit to the standard established by the Passive House Institute US (PHIUS). A passive house is

- Superinsulated

- Thoroughly air sealed

- Properly ventilated, using either a heat-recovery ventilator (HRV) or an energy-recovery ventilator (ERV)

- Outfitted with high-performance windows and doors

- Mindful of eliminating thermal bridges

- Oriented and organized to take advantage of solar and internal heat gains

For Jen and Brian, one of the perks of pursuing the passive house retrofit is the resulting small heating/cooling system. "We have the ERV closet, and then we have a mini split on each floor, and beyond that there are no baseboards or big mechanical room with furnaces, so that gave us more space," notes Jen.

The horizontal slatted guard rail picks up on the theme of horizontal details throughout the house and contributes to the sense of airiness.

Tall ceilings also help to relieve some of the row house's narrowness, and, of course, partially open stairs provide relief as well. A horizontal slatted guard-rail design picks up on the long horizontal of the plan, the kitchen island, and the straight stairs. It allows users to perceive both party walls, which makes the house feel wider. The horizontal design of the guard rail is also echoed in the horizontal planking of oversize closet doors in the master bedroom, the oversize sliding door to Lilly's room, and on the storage wall in Levi's room. "Because it's a small house broken up into floors, we wanted to have a similar language throughout the house to connect them," Jen explains.

They chose not to extend the house any farther back on the lot to preserve daylight front to back but also so they could enjoy a more generous site-sensitive backyard. The property is 100 ft. deep, and the house occupies 41 ft. 6 in. of the front depth, which leaves 58 ft. 6 in. for the rear. After repeatedly attempting to grow grass unsuccessfully out back, they opted

 Because the ceiling in Levi's room is so tall, the horizontal wall paneling helps bring the scale of the space down for a child. The door blends into the wall for an uncluttered effect.

 Taking advantage of available space over the stairs, the shelving in Lilly's room maximizes storage and creates a pocket for privacy.

for an area of highly durable AstroTurf instead, which the kids enjoy playing and lounging on. "It's made it another room," marvels Jen. Plus, from inside the living area, "You feel like that outdoor space is part of the room." she continues.

In the design of their own house, Jen and Brian were thrilled to have the opportunity to test the many interventions that architects often recommend to others. Much to their pleasure, the tricks of the trade really worked. "The quality of the light and the clarity of the air make the whole experience in the house really delightful," Jen concludes.

The door to daughter Lilly's room is 8 ft. tall and shares the horizontal planking detail seen in her brother's room. The stairs from the third floor offer a view of the rear yard and provide a glimpse of the living room below through the slot in the second floor.

FAMILY ADU

SITE   3D   DAYLIGHT   BIG/SMALL   MULTI-PURPOSE   PRIVACY   IN/OUT   FINISH PALETTE   QUALITY MATERIALS   DETAILS

We kept the plan utterly simple.

WHAT A DIFFERENCE innovative zoning can make! In 2010, Portland, Oreg., eased permitting regulations and fees for accessory dwelling units (ADUs), which are smaller second dwelling units (often referred to as "granny flats") on lots that also contain a house. Sized at a maximum of 800 sq. ft. or 75% of the size of the primary dwelling, whichever is smaller, ADUs offer an affordable housing alternative that can readily be woven into existing neighborhoods. When a savvy Realtor® suggested to James Michelinie and Kyra Routon-Michelinie that the home they had

The cedar arbor adds a distinctive detail, while shading and providing filtered privacy to the gable-end custom window/door assembly, which makes a big statement on the small house.

been renting—on a corner lot with a garage—and were considering purchasing would be a prime candidate for an ADU, the young couple started imagining the possibilities.

When Kyra was growing up, her architect father, Steve Routon, and her mother, Darro, led the family in many home renovations and, apparently, passed the renovation/building bug onto their middle daughter. "It was always kind of a dream that I had wanted my entire life to build a home with my parents and with my husband," says Kyra. She and James figured they could save on labor expenses if they framed and finished the house with Kyra's parents' help. They also liked the idea that, after constructing the ADU, they could move into it and rent out the 2,000 sq.-ft. main house. When they start a family of their own, they plan to move back into the main house. Kyra's parents, who have a house in Oregon's northwest coastal range, will then use the ADU—in which they will have invested more than sweat equity—as their in-town house.

The Douglas fir–trimmed front window/door wall climbs toward the ridge nearly 19 ft. above the concrete floor, which acquired a warm patina during construction and acts as a heat sink. Kyra made the muslin curtains that offer some privacy in the evenings and soften light during the day.

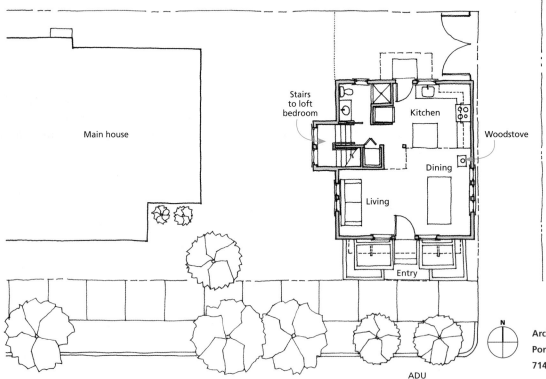

Main house

Stairs to loft bedroom

Kitchen

Woodstove

Dining

Living

Entry

ADU

N

Architect: Steven Routon
Portland, Oreg.
714 sq. ft.

Kyra and James do most of their entertaining in the open kitchen/dining area. The construction-grade Douglas fir stair enclosure, loft guard rail, and the distinctive interior arbor, which supports the stair landing, add texture and warmth to the sage-green walls.

The team initially planned to renovate the existing garage into an ADU, but when it proved not to be salvageable, Steve began sketches for a new building instead. Beyond regulating size and yard setbacks, the zoning required an onsite parking space to replace the one the garage had provided. And Steve wanted to maximize space between the two dwellings on the 4,000-sq.-ft. lot to shape a site-sensitive outdoor room. So in response to those constraints and a tight budget, "We kept the plan utterly simple," says Steve. It's nearly square with a bump for the stair landing to the west and few interior walls.

The multipurpose open kitchen, dining/living area on the first floor accounts for 520 sq. ft., features a woodstove, and includes only one interior passage door to the full bathroom and a door to the laundry closet. The 194-sq.-ft. loft bedroom above is open to below and borrows daylight from the southern window wall at the entrance to the house, while providing a pocket for privacy. The loft location above the kitchen and bathroom lends those spaces a lower 8-ft. ceiling and renders them more intimate.

The south-facing window wall (mostly custom built by Steve) in the gable end on the street garners a fair amount of attention and is arguably the biggest statement the small house makes. It welcomes abundant daylight into the open interior, invites the sun to heat the concrete floors (which in turn gradually release heat to the house), and actively engages with passersby on the street, which the city has designated as a bike boulevard. "If you're an extravert, it's really a great place to live because there are no strangers. Everybody seems to have taken possession of the house since it has such a relationship to the street," says Steve. Stepped planters along the

 The loft bedroom overlooks the front living space, from which it borrows daylight and a sense of expansiveness.

front and a distinctive arbor built into the window wall provide a buffer. Grape vines climbing the arbor offer a veil of privacy and some shading from the sun in the heat of the day.

Inside, the distinctive detail of the exterior arbor is echoed by the structure supporting the stair landing. Steve refers to it as an interior arbor. "I wanted to continue the garden theme," he says, and bring the outdoors in. While the exterior arbor and window wall are high-quality cedar, the interior arbor, stair enclosure, and window trim are more affordable construction-grade Douglas fir. Steve envisioned the stairs as a sculptural element in the otherwise somewhat austere interior that would serve the additional purposes of concealing the laundry closet, storage, and entrance to the full bath. "It's a small house; you don't want to see everything from the living space. So I really wanted to tuck the stairs behind," he explains.

The Douglas fir–clad stairs provide a dynamic center piece while concealing several fundamental support functions: the laundry closet, storage, and the entrance to the bathroom.

 Custom fixed windows (also made by Steve) are located at transom height above the modest open sitting area and offer privacy while bringing in western light. Because the sitting area is narrower than the dining area and bordered by the stair enclosure, it provides a pocket for privacy from the hubbub in the dining/kitchen area.

 Flow through and around the kitchen was critical to Kyra and James. Black walnut kitchen cabinet faces were selected to relate to the black walnut dining table and to contrast the birch butcher-block counters.

The flow and function of the kitchen were critical to Kyra and James. "We spend a disproportionate amount of our time cooking," notes James. So the kitchen is somewhat large (12 ft. 3 in. by 9 ft. 6 in.), considering the overall size of their small house; and like the bathroom, the kitchen can be a big-ticket expense. "Building a small house per square foot is obviously really expensive relative to building a larger house where you amortize those spaces," notes Steve. And since budget was an issue, Kyra and James chose IKEA birch butcher-block countertops and IKEA cabinet boxes, drawers, and hardware. They invested a bit more in custom cabinet faces of black walnut that resemble the custom black-walnut dining table that James's brother, Pete Michelinie, made the couple for a wedding gift.

Kyra and James will miss the ADU when they move back into the main house, and Steve and Darro are looking forward to occupying it. They will all be thrilled to be close by each other when Kyra and James welcome their first child into the family. It's no surprise that such a flexible new small-house paradigm like the ADU is catching on.

The horizontal composition of the IKEA birch butcher-block island top and counters, which Kyra and James selected in part for their affordability, relates to the horizontal skip sheathing used on the stair enclosure.

 Sometimes a design is shaped by accommodating a prized possession or family heirloom, like the custom black walnut dining table that James's brother made the couple for a wedding gift, which was included in all of Steve's early sketches for the ADU. The nearby woodstove is the house's primary heating source.

 Steve conceived of the stair enclosure finish as horizontal board and batten where it encloses closet space and horizontal slatted arbor trellis where it serves as a guard rail. He and the family-framing-and-finish team ripped, sanded, and sealed every piece of the construction-grade Douglas fir skip sheathing.

VICTORIAN MODERN

| SITE | 3D | DAYLIGHT | BIG/SMALL | MULTI-PURPOSE | PRIVACY | IN/OUT | FINISH PALETTE | QUALITY MATERIALS | DETAILS |

It is a very tightly designed micro house.

IT WAS THE SMALL RETREAT behind the house that architect Ted Chapin renovated for himself and Torrence Boone in Provincetown, Massachusetts, that initially caught my attention. I was visiting Provincetown for the first time, padding the streets, camera in hand, enthralled by the historic fabric of interlocking properties, pocket gardens, and whimsical structures. The little "barn," as Ted calls it, was peeking out across the extensive flagstone patio practically begging me to take a picture of its fish-scale-like copper roof, four-panel French doors, and diminutive deck that appears to float above a small Koi pond. I went so far as to mostly crop Ted and Torrence's dark-purple, mid-19th century house from the foreground of the barn photo because the house fit so quietly into the streetscape that I hardly noticed it.

 Set close to the street, the antique gambrel includes an enclosed porch that currently serves as a sunny sitting space with a small roof deck above. The "barn" retreat peeks out from across the flagstone, a material that Ted describes as "the glue that holds all of the property together."

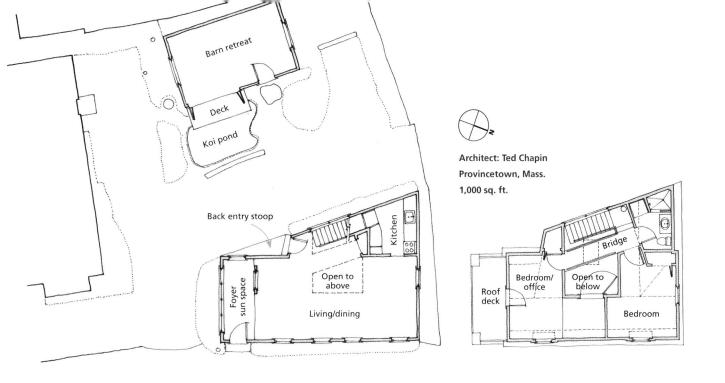

Barn retreat

Deck

Koi pond

Back entry stoop

Foyer sun space

Kitchen

Open to above

Living/dining

Architect: Ted Chapin
Provincetown, Mass.
1,000 sq. ft.

Roof deck

Bedroom/office

Open to below

Bridge

Bedroom

The copper roofing material on the barn retreat matches the copper siding on the back of the house. "I wanted the two buildings to have a dialogue," notes Ted. The four-panel French doors open to a small deck that hovers above a koi pond (where a small addition once stood).

The footprint of the angled rear wall predated Ted's renovation. It contained a one-story kitchen. Ted extended the wall up to maximize interior space and introduced the angled seam of wall finishes that intersects the large square window.

That's the thing about Ted and Torrence's house; if you didn't know better, you might think it was merely a sweet Victorian-era gambrel cottage. But it's so much more. This becomes evident when you walk around the back to the wedge of a deck that is the entry stoop and discover the contemporary two-story rear elevation. On it, a large square window divided into four smaller squares is intersected by a diagonal seam where purple-painted shingles meet copper interlocking fish–scale like panels. It's a bold, distinctive graphic composition that signals a more modern sensibility and makes a big statement on a small house.

Because the house is in a historic district, Ted maintained an antique appearance on its three public faces. However, on the interior and the fourth face, which looks inward at the more private courtyard, he chose to freely express a fresh attitude toward today's living. He doesn't object to the requirements of the Historic District Commission–quite

"There were already a lot of diagonals on the building," Ted explains. The angled seam where the copper interlocking siding meets the shingle siding is drawn from the angle of the house's gambrel roof. "It grows out of the existing architecture," continues Ted.

the contrary; he credits the Historic District Commission with saving the town. "They kept a lid on it so things were sensitively restored," he explains. He worked within the commission's framework to create a unique home of its place and time.

Step inside the rear entry of Ted's house, and you find yourself in a multipurpose open living/dining space. Straight ahead lies a sculptural maple staircase, which follows the angle of the exterior wall, as does the maple flooring. A few steps farther inside brings you beneath the second-floor bridge, which also follows the angle of the exterior stairs,

and a few more steps brings you to the heart of the two-story atrium awash in daylight from a skylight above. You can't help but look up and experience a release from the lower ceilings that edge the first floor.

Farther ahead, tucked in behind the stairs, is a small kitchen niche, largely out of sight. It's a functional IKEA kitchen with a splashy Indian marble floor (which also makes an appearance in the front sitting space and bathroom). "Bear in mind: the bathroom, the bedroom, the kitchen are small; it's almost like living in a cabin cruiser. It is a very tightly designed micro house," says Ted. Micro though it may be,

 The open living/dining space has a lower ceiling along the perimeter, a two-story atrium toward the middle that's edged by a sculptural staircase made of maple (like the floors), and a second-floor bridge that connects the bedrooms.

 The foyer sun space sits outside a remnant of the one-time exterior wall that Ted preserved. He kept the original window in place, offering an interior view of the larger space beyond. A unique angled shingle pattern edges the foyer's maple door jamb, which picks up on the many angles in the house and the local practice of applying shingle patterns on exterior walls.

From the living/dining room side of the foyer sun space, the angled plaster wall intersection with the maple wall of the door jamb recalls the angle of the gambrel roof in much the same fashion as the angled seam of copper and wooden shingles on the rear exterior wall.

A trapezoidal door beneath the stairs conceals a small coat closet, while a flush hatch in the floor provides access to a partial crawl space that contains mechanical equipment. Zinc terrazzo divider strips edge the floor hatch and contribute to an overall floor pattern; the divider strip that's parallel to the angled wall and stairs continues to the border of the sun space on axis with the view down the street to the water.

The view from Torrence's desk in the second bedroom, which serves as his part-time office, extends across the bridge and out the enormous rear window toward Provincetown's iconic Pilgrim Monument in the distance.

Ted designed quiet pockets for privacy along the periphery to take in the roomier more public spaces, while enjoying a slight remove from them, which allows the small house to feel more spacious. The front sitting alcove, which is technically the foyer, is a great example. Set just beyond a reimagined remnant of an exterior wall with an interior stained-glass double-hung window in its original location, the intimate sun space is close to the street and open living/dining space but slightly buffered from both. Ted called for the front face of the remnant wall to be shingled as a reminder that it was once an exterior wall, which lends the alcove a porch-like presence.

You could argue that the second-floor bridge acts in a somewhat similar fashion as a pocket for privacy. It's both part of the open common living space and slightly buffered from it by virtue of its position overhead. Ted notes, "The building feels so big for its size, and it never feels bigger than when you're walking across that bridge." The same could be said for the flagstone-patio courtyard/outdoor room in the midst of the buildings that Ted renovated. From the patio, the modest compound, including the barn retreat that initially drew me to the property, feels utterly commodious in part because the retreat offers another pocket for privacy from which to enjoy the property and bring the outdoors in. The retreat, once Ted's studio, now serves as an on-site getaway. The inventive variety of spaces and the experiences they offer, thanks to Ted's design, allow his renovated small house and its surrounds to live unexpectedly large.

 A small roof deck off the office extends living space outdoors and offers a view of the town, including a glimpse of the barn retreat roof and the library steeple beyond. Ted and Torrence often sit out on the deck and greet friends and neighbors. "It's like a little front porch," says Ted.

 Used as a violin-making workshop by a previous owner, the retreat served as Ted's art studio for a while, but now he and Torrence use it more as a place to relax. The ship's ladder and salvaged wood interior finish are original to the retreat; Ted opened up the second floor to give the space a lift similar to the atrium in the house. Ted says the retreat is the yin to the yang of the house.

THE SAMUEL NOAKES HOUSE ANEW

SITE   3D   DAYLIGHT   BIG/SMALL   MULTI-PURPOSE   FINISH PALETTE   QUALITY MATERIALS

We mined the building to find the historic stuff.

LIVING IN A SMALL apartment in a renovated antique building is a unique experience. I know; my husband and I used to live in a two-level condo in a 1768 Georgian home in Salem, Mass. We relished padding upon the original wide pine floors and warming by the massive central brick chimney, while also taking advantage of modern amenities like an updated kitchen and baths. It was a symmetrical building logically arranged that divided relatively simply into four units accessed from central stairs that climbed three floors in what was once a sea captain's home. The 1810 Samuel Noakes House in

The Levi Wickham house, on the left, is where John lived before buying and renovating the Samuel Noakes House, on the right, which fronts Braddock Street. For years, the first-floor basement storefront in the Samuel Noakes House was a barbershop.

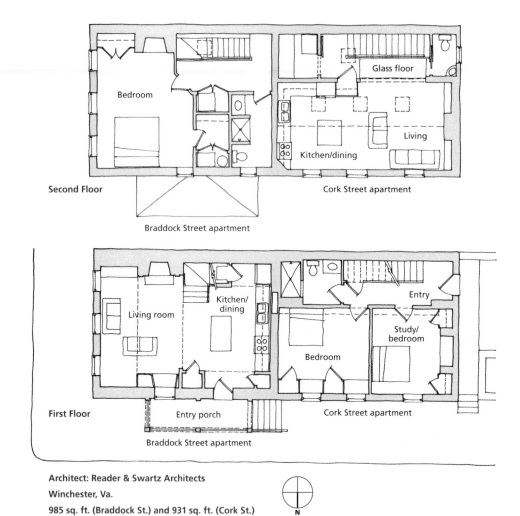

Second Floor

Bedroom

Glass floor

Kitchen/dining

Living

Cork Street apartment

Braddock Street apartment

First Floor

Living room

Kitchen/dining

Entry

Study/bedroom

Bedroom

Entry porch

Cork Street apartment

Braddock Street apartment

Architect: Reader & Swartz Architects
Winchester, Va.
985 sq. ft. (Braddock St.) and 931 sq. ft. (Cork St.)

N

The 1840 rear addition facing Cork Street, where John lives, is the apartment (blue with green shutters) with the backyard. The original 1810 front section facing Braddock Street is the other apartment (red). It includes the porch facing Cork Street

 The open multipurpose dining/living area on the first floor of the Braddock Street apartment enjoys daylight and views out tall windows. A bead-board soffit linking the fireplace wall on one end and built-ins for storage on the other accommodates structure and ductwork while providing a visual threshold between spaces.

Winchester, Va., however, proved to be far more challenging to convert into two quality small apartments for today's professionals. It's not symmetrical; its layout was illogical, and it had fallen into a state of disrepair. None of this deterred John Chesson, who owned and occupied the renovated limestone building next door known as the Levi Wickham House, from buying the Samuel Noakes House as well.

The front of the Samuel Noakes House faces Braddock Street and was once a small one-and-a-half-story stone building that included street-level basement access. Then, sometime around 1840 the house was altered. The roof was raised to capture additional headroom and daylight through new short windows, a brick facade was introduced on the front, and a two-story brick addition was added to the rear extending along Cork Street. The result was essentially two buildings that shared neither floor levels nor ceiling heights, but were tenuously connected through a party wall.

  A skylight above the refinished original stairs washes the white bead-board wall with daylight to be shared with the dining/kitchen area. A clear-finished section of original bead board is visible beneath the stairs bounding the pantry.

A previous owner had divided the house horizontally into two low-rent apartments stacked one on top of the other, and a barbershop occupied the walk-out basement. The rooms in both apartments were poorly organized and subject to sound disturbance from either the apartment above or below. Plus, basic infrastructure was lacking; the majority of the electrical wiring ran along the exterior of the uninsulated building that was heated with electric baseboards. On the advice of his

From the sizable second-floor bedroom in the Braddock Street apartment, the succinct finish palette—including the original pine wood floors, exposed brick party wall, white bead-board built-ins, and light green walls—is on display.

 Upstairs, the glass floor marks entry to the multipurpose space and is surrounded by bamboo floors. The horizontal steel-rod stair balustrade emphasizes the length of the space and allows views through it to the richly textured party wall from the adjacent open multipurpose space.

In the entry stair hall of the Cork Street apartment, the modern materials of the new steel stairs and glass floor above contrast with the reclaimed stained pine treads and exposed original masonry of the party wall. The skylight and glass floor draw you forward and up to the more public living level upstairs and make a big statement for a small apartment.

architects Beth Reader and Chuck Schwartz, John decided to divide the house vertically at the party wall, between the original front of the house and the rear addition, into two more functional and efficient apartments. The vertical separation of the apartments would give each better sound privacy, direct access to grade, and improve fire separation between the apartments. "Each apartment was to have its own outdoor space. So the one unit would have the Cork Street porch and the other unit would have the backyard outside space," notes Beth. "We were trying to make something that makes sense for more modern demographics," explains Chuck.

Because the front apartment on Braddock Street had taller windows on the main level above the basement storefront and shorter windows on the second floor, the team designated the first floor the more public level to accommodate a multi-purpose kitchen/dining/living area and the second floor a more private level for the bedroom and bathroom. They made the opposite designations on the rear apartment that fronts Cork Street. Again paying attention to the third dimension, they decided to locate a more public multipurpose kitchen/dining/living area on the second floor, where it could take advantage of cathedral ceiling space beneath the gable

 Custom built-in drawers and cabinets around the windows in John's first-floor bedroom replace the need for a bureau or conventional closet, which can take up precious space in a small apartment. The clean, grooved design is a contemporary take on the house's original board-and-batten doors. The cork floor provides a warm accent as do the partially exposed stained floor joists above, which allow for a slightly higher ceiling.

roof, and a more private level for two bedrooms and a bathroom on the first floor under lower ceilings.

The property is in a historic district, so the architects did little to modify the exterior other than repair or replace materials in kind, install new insulated double-glazed windows and new skylights (not visible from the street), and make some other small improvements. The team had freer rein on the interior, since they decided to forgo potential federal and state rehabilitation tax credits and because the interior is outside of the historic district's purview. "We basically mined the building to find the historic stuff," says Chuck. They

decided they would expose existing masonry on party walls when appropriate and expose floor framing where it might be advantageous to increase visual interest or apparent ceiling height. The exterior walls would be framed out on the interior with 2×4s to accommodate insulation and infrastructure, like wiring and plumbing.

Following the lead of the entry porch design on Cork Street, the small apartment facing Braddock Street has a more traditional interior aesthetic. The original stairs were maintained and refinished as were the original floors, when possible. The open kitchen/dining/living area enjoys a succinct finish palette of mostly white bead board and custom mill-work; light putty colored walls and stained kitchen cabinets; and accents of black leathered granite countertops, exposed masonry, and floor framing. A large skylight above the stairs lends daylight to the kitchen/dining area, the staircase, and the second floor. Windows on both sides of the living area provide additional daylight and views of the streetscape visible from each of the overlapping spaces in the open room.

The small apartment facing Cork Street required a more inventive interior solution since it lacked serviceable existing stairs and had fewer and smaller windows overall, which led to a more contemporary interior aesthetic. Beneath a skylight in the Cork Street apartment, Beth and Chuck designed a section of glass flooring for the second-floor stair hall, which makes a big statement in this small apartment. "I liked the idea of not walking into a little cavern and being able to look up and see the space that you were about to enter. And it made sense from a light standpoint," notes John. The steel-framed glass floor led to the design of a steel stair. Upstairs in the open kitchen/dining/living space, attention to the third

The open dining area and contemporary kitchen benefit from skylights above and views across the stair hall that seemingly enlarge the multipurpose space.

 A cased opening off the stair hall provides wide access to the open dining/living area beneath exposed original rafter ties that buffer the height of the cathedral ceiling without compromising it. Built-ins on the exterior wall provide neat and functional space on either side of the concealed chimney traveling up from below.

dimension in the form of the cathedral ceiling and south-facing skylights allows the multipurpose space to feel generous and bright. The updated finish palette includes bamboo floors, white walls, a shiplap board-finished cathedral ceiling, and full-overlay cabinets; details like painted green millwork, stained exposed rafter ties, and areas of exposed masonry further define the aesthetic.

When the project was complete, John was so enamored with the small apartment facing Cork Street that he moved in, downsizing from the neighboring Levi Wickham house. "In

my case, it's comforting. It's not big and echoey . . . Built into all of that, it's hyperpractical space; everything has its place," says John. He concludes, "I also like the idea that if we all lived in slightly smaller spaces, we'd have a lot more room for everything else."

EASTIE VERSATILITY

SITE 3D DAYLIGHT BIG/ MULTI- PRIVACY IN/OUT FINISH QUALITY DETAILS
SMALL PURPOSE PALETTE MATERIALS

FROM THE STREET, you'd never guess that behind the diminutive green façade of this house in East Boston (known as Eastie to locals) lies a versatile, free-flowing, bright floor-through. Subtle moves like the flared siding over the entry only hint at the interior wonders of architect Lyle Bradley's family home. Small front windows provide privacy, saving the surprise of the multipurpose interior and its connection to the multipurpose rear yard for those lucky enough to be invited inside in person (or via the pages of this book).

> I had the most fun designing and building the stairs.

Clad with green HardiePlank, Lyle and Kara's house features casement windows composed of salvaged sashes from double-hung windows that Lyle hung sideways, which orients the muntins horizontally. He modeled the window operation on windows he observed during a semester in Finland. An outer casement swings out; an inner casement swings in and contains a panel of glass that can be swapped out for a screen.

 Viewed from just steps within the entry, the wrapping stair risers and horizontal patterning of the western built-in wall draw your eye through the open living/dining/kitchen and out to the greenhouse and hint of the yard beyond. Fir floors, stair treads, and ceiling trim unite the space, while maple and birch components provide accents to the white walls and ceiling. The pendant light fixture is the Coral Pendant by David Trubridge.

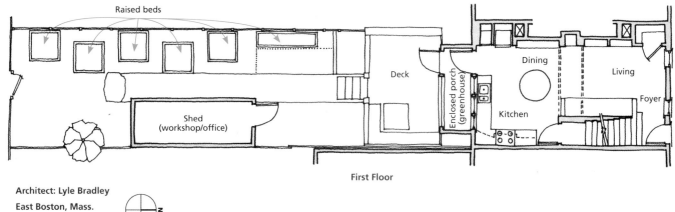

Raised beds

Shed (workshop/office)

Deck

Enclosed porch (greenhouse)

Dining

Living

Foyer

Kitchen

First Floor

Architect: Lyle Bradley
East Boston, Mass.
800 sq. ft.

A staircase like no other is washed in daylight from the monitor above and accommodates a built-in couch. It has a sculptural presence—it's not surprising to learn that Lyle's concentration while an undergrad art major was sculpture.

A MULTIPURPOSE STAIR THAT MAKES ALL THE DIFFERENCE

"I had the most fun designing and building the stairs... There's so much action that happens around any stair, and I think this one has maybe a little bit more action," says Lyle. Not only does the stairway provide a means of traveling between floor levels, it channels daylight, bows like the hull of a boat, and shapes a built-in living-area couch.

With attention to the third dimension, Lyle designed a roof monitor above the stairs featuring skylight windows on three sides that also flood Lily's room and the first-floor living area with daylight. The fourth western side of the monitor is solid so as to prevent late afternoon sun from overheating the house.

The bowed boatlike sidewall of the stairs, under the built-in desk in Lily's room, is a nod to the neighborhood's former boatbuilding industry. Horizontal battens suggest boat planking while relating to the distinctive horizontal millwork elements on the first floor. The plane of the bowed wall is further suggested in the risers that slide behind the built-in couch and provide a gradually reclining backrest. The third tread wraps to become an armrest.

Shelves in niches receive as much design attention as a radiator enclosure and are modeled on the Japanese tokonoma. The staggered maple shelves and maple trim establish an emphasis on horizontal elements that appears in other details and reinforce the horizontal nature of the open first floor.

Lyle routed horizontal slots in birch plywood and wove fir strips vertically through them to create a panel that slides like a shoji screen to reveal bar storage on one end and a radiator on the other.

When Lyle acquired his row house he recognized that the existing stair layout had broken the house's design. The stairs ran parallel to the front and rear of the house and divided the front living area from the kitchen and rear yard, effectively cutting the house in half. In order for the house's 15-ft. by 30-ft. footprint to live larger, Lyle knew he would need to create an open, multipurpose space that flowed from the northern street entrance toward a glassy southern rear wall and out to the garden beyond, so he removed the existing stairs and designed new stairs along the eastern party wall directly off the entrance. With that significant alteration, Lyle began transforming his house into a series of new multipurpose solutions.

Today, two parallel beam soffits, trimmed at the bottom with fir, are reminders on the primary living level of where the stairs were. "The first floor is a foyer, a living room, a kitchen, and a dining room," notes Lyle, and those soffits help subtly define one area from the other without dividing them.

 From the back alley gate, capped with an arched flourish Lyle made, the Japanese-influenced shed and landscaping lead past verdant planters constructed of 4×4 fir to the deck and greenhouse rear entrance. The bluestone and field rocks were all salvaged.

 Atop the green roof of the greenhouse, the green roof of the shed is visible. "I think if every house had a green roof, it would make a big difference," says Lyle who is concerned about the cumulative effect of contaminants in water runoff, the heat-island effect of so many black roofs, and the loss of plant life in the city.

In addition, they help mitigate the length of the somewhat low ceiling, by interrupting it. Otherwise the space might feel more tunnel-like.

On the western wall, Lyle took advantage of some existing recesses and created others to receive new built-ins that serve a variety of purposes that reflect a combination of boatlike and Japanese craftsmanship, while playing on the horizontal nature of the now open space. "I'm a wood guy, so boats and Japanese architecture sort of epitomize master craft in wood-working," says Lyle who studied at the Center for Furniture Craftsmanship in Maine before attending architecture school. The distinctive detail of staggered maple shelves, which is also echoed in the staggered maple treatment of the radiator enclosure near the entrance, was inspired by the traditional Japanese tokonoma. "That is an alcove found in a lot of Japanese houses meant for cherished objects and often found near the entry of a house," he explains. Lyle's interpretations accommodate display items, books, the TV, and, well, a radiator.

Farther down the western wall, closer to the kitchen area, is another built-in with a distinctive horizontal emphasis. A panel face composed of seemingly woven birch plywood and fir slides like a shoji screen in either direction to reveal alternately bar bottles and glasses or another radiator. In a small house, such versatile, dynamic built-in storage solutions add interest and are key to maintaining an uncluttered, free-flowing open space.

The dining deck is bordered by a tall wall finished with the same reeds that Lyle bought by the roll for the exterior panels in his workshop/office. Eastie's triple deckers beyond are a reminder of the house's urban context.

Horizontal fir strips, like the horizontal maple shelves and trim elements in the living area, wrap panels of reeds and painted plywood on the shed. Inexpensive Polygal carbonate sheets admit filtered daylight into Lyle's workshop/office.

Lily's room in the space that was originally conceived of as an office contains a sizable desk that she may use someday for homework. Daylight from the adjacent stairs and stair hall give her room an airy quality.

Toward the rear of the first floor, a French patio door opens onto the "greenhouse," as Lyle calls it, where an exterior French patio door that Lyle salvaged from a job site flanks a repurposed slider door (from a neighbor) that Lyle turned sideways to function as oversize windows. The kitchen and living area borrow daylight and view from the greenhouse, which serves a number of purposes: seed-starting area, recycling center, and mudroom. It's an ancillary space that transitions to the outdoor dining deck and the deep backyard. There, Lyle's Japanese-inspired workshop/office offers a pocket for privacy and edges an outdoor room that is also bound by fencing and partially populated with raised-bed planters that he and his wife, Kara Lashley, designed in collaboration.

On the second floor, two-year-old daughter Lily's room abuts the stairs in a space that Lyle originally conceived of as an office, with a built-in desk sized for two, and spillover guest quarters. Interior openings above the low desk wall and a cased opening off the stair hall give the room breathing space and allow it to borrow daylight from the monitor above the stair. Lyle notes that if Lily ever wanted her room enclosed, he would likely fill the interior openings with Polygal™ polycarbonate sheets, the same material he used in his backyard workshop/office, and hang a door in the cased opening.

Anticipating how to modify spaces as needs change is indicative of the type of thinking that enabled Lyle to imagine a multifaceted, open, and sunny home that reaches deep into a series of successively engaging and lush outdoor living spaces. Hidden behind many an unassuming in-town rowhouse exterior is a small-house solution waiting to be realized.

The boatlike bow of the stair sidewall is Lyle's nod to Eastie's boatbuilding past. Its detailing also picks up on the horizontal trim theme seen elsewhere in the house. The three-sided monitor above gives the space a thrilling lift, while filling it with daylight.

NEW ENGLAND COTTAGE COURT

SITE 3D DAYLIGHT MULTI-PURPOSE PRIVACY IN/OUT FINISH PALETTE QUALITY MATERIALS

It looks like some version of the American Dream.

NEW URBANIST ARCHITECT Donald Powers of Union Studio had been eying the 0.85-acre lot occupied by a moribund auto-repair place in the heart of East Greenwich, R.I., while he was living nearby. He thought the location might be ideal for a densely sited community of new, small, mixed-income, cottage-like condominiums occupying an area between commercial main street and neighboring single-family homes. The resulting Cottages on Greene, which he designed and developed as a minority partner, is a compact cottage-court community of 15 small two-bedroom units, some attached, some freestanding (including 5 affordable units) arranged around a common green.

The human scale of front porches and one-and a-half-story gabled forms arranged around a common green and clad with traditional residential finishes is the hallmark of this new cottage court community. "It looks like some version of the American Dream: a little house on its own plot of land," says Don.

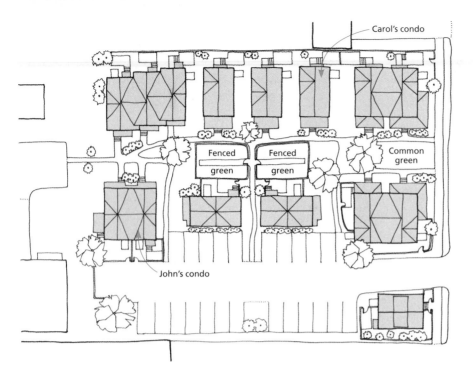

Carol's condo

Fenced green

Fenced green

Common green

John's condo

Architect: Union Studio
East Greenwich, R.I.
1,094 sq. ft. and 878 sq. ft.

"In my mind, the primary defining nature of these pocket neighborhoods or cottage courts is that they focus on a common space, as opposed to being a single building with space around it. They create a sense of community and the opportunity for community, by organizing themselves around a public realm," notes Don. The central court acts in many ways as a site-sensitive series of outdoor rooms, some edged by picket fences others by foot paths. With the aid of new urbanist planner and civil engineer Jon Ford, then of Morris Beacon Design, the court and other spaces between and around buildings also manage storm water on site. "We had an attitude that we weren't going to build any infrastructure that didn't add to the cuteness of the place," says Don. So a series of drainage spillways, depressions, and swales are woven into the design with little bridges and pathways that enhance the journey between the units.

There are variations of two plan types knit into the community layout. Freestanding units toward the center of the court are flanked by duplexes and a triplex anchoring the corners. The small, one-and-a-half-story cottage designs express a single-family scale, even when units are attached, because gable fronts allow each unit to be read separately. John McDonald lives in one of the plan types in a duplex. His condo features a multipurpose first-floor open plan that

Front gables such as those on the duplex John occupies help the units to be understood separately, even though they're attached. The porch of John's unit is illuminated and brimming with potted plants and hanging baskets.

 From John's porch, the view down the length of the central court and past the cottage units that line it belies the size of the small, densely sited community. Picket fences in the court and little Trex® bridges connecting footpaths across drainage beds add charm and neighborliness.

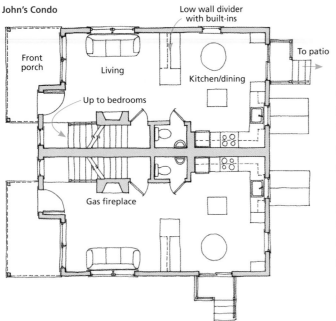

John's Condo

Low wall divider with built-ins

Front porch

Living

Kitchen/dining

To patio

Up to bedrooms

Gas fireplace

includes a low dividing partition that houses bookshelves on the living-room side and a desk or email station on the kitchen/dining side with a base cabinet occupying the end. "I like the open space," John says. And he appreciates how the low wall suggests a separation between the living and dining/kitchen areas while still allowing a borrowed view across the spaces and out the rear glass sliders to the back patio. The wall also defines a pocket for privacy on either side. "Having it feel large is more a matter of accommodating several different kinds of living experiences than it is so much about having enormous space," notes Don.

The small front porch and back patio are two more spaces that help deliver the different kinds of living experiences to

A low wall between the living and dining/kitchen area in John's unit helps differentiate one area from the other. Across the top, the low wall allows one space to borrow daylight from the other and for the view to extend all of the way through the open multipurpose space, which makes the first floor feel larger. Built-in shelving adds additional function to the low wall.

A desk/email station built into the low wall on the dining/kitchen side provides a pocket for privacy within the overall open plan. The succinct interior finish palette of white woodwork, off-white walls, and red oak floors contributes to the fluidity of one area to the next, yielding a sense of spaciousness.

The cross-gable dormer on the side of John's unit fronts an access path leading from the community parking area. His duplex features red cedar accents that enhance the community's succinct exterior finish palette.

NEW URBANISM NOW

The new urbanism movement got under way in the 1980s in response to increasing widespread suburban sprawl, originally spawned by the post-1950 American romance with the car. New urbanism promotes walkable, compact, human-scaled, mixed-use, sustainable, and traditionally structured neighborhoods, communities, and cities organized around shared public spaces that enhance connections between a diversity of people and activities, creating a sense of place. The Congress of New Urbanism, a nonprofit organization formed in 1993, promotes new urbanist principles and advocates for development practices and public policy friendly to new urbanism.

After the U.S. housing collapse and Great Recession of 2008, new urbanists like architect Don Powers were eager to take action. "I got into sort of fever pitch to help reinvent the new model, and I wasn't alone. All the new urbanist architects were gathering to say, 'How are we going to respond to this?' " explains Don. Cottages on Greene was Don's initial answer to that question. He is quick to note that precedents for new urbanist housing models like Cottages on Greene can be found in the California bungalow courts of the 1920s and 1930s as well as the Toronto and Philadelphia worker's cottages of the late 19th century. "For those of us who have been studying it, it's dusting off a housing model that got left behind after the automobile," says Don.

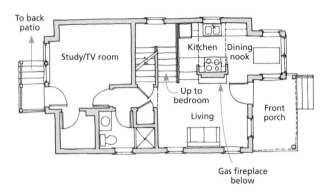

Study/TV room

To back patio

Kitchen

Dining nook

Up to bedroom

Living

Front porch

Gas fireplace below

Carol's freestanding unit features a dining nook bay that sidles up to her front porch. Though her house is a different color than her neighbors', the exterior finish palette of HardiePlank and HardiePanel® siding, white trim, and asphalt-shingle roofing help tie her unit in with the others, creating a coherent larger community, while the color variation from one unit to the next allows for orchestrated variety.

which Don refers. John enjoys bringing the indoors out and the outdoors in by grilling on his back patio during the more temperate months and sitting on his northwest-facing front porch on summer mornings when it's cooler under the shading roof. He has two bedrooms upstairs, one of which is outfitted for guests and houses his desktop computer. "Invariably, when my son and daughter come to visit at the same time or my son and his girlfriend, one of them will be sitting at the kitchen table with maybe two of us watching TV, and somebody else will be upstairs on the Internet," says John. He continues, "There's plenty of room and that much more in the summer because I've got the back patio, and I've got the front porch."

Carol Donatelli lives in the other plan type. Her unit is freestanding and contains a multipurpose living/kitchen/dining semiopen plan beneath a cathedral ceiling. She notes

that when women visitors enter the space, "They all look up and say, 'Oh, this is so beautiful.'" The men, she says, are very charmed with the full basement, which is big enough to store Carol's dining set among other furnishings from her previous larger home in North Providence, the town where she and her husband (who has since passed away) raised a family of seven children and lived for 55 years. She may move the dining set to the living level someday if she plans on hosting a large, special-occasion meal. In the meantime, she enjoys breakfasts in the intimate niche pocket for privacy off the open kitchen, facing the exterior court, and other meals in the front open living area by the gas fireplace.

A back room that she uses as a study/TV room on the first floor could alternatively function as a first-floor bedroom since it's adjacent to a full bath and walk-in closet. "In the evening it's very secluded back there. . . . I have a little dog,

 The height of the cathedral ceiling in the multipurpose semiopen plan makes the place look much larger than the square footage would suggest. "And it just gives you a nice open feeling," says Carol.

 Carol sits at a high table in the breakfast/dining nook, a pocket for privacy where she can comfortably see out windows on three sides and back into the kitchen. Her Maltese, Sacci, looks ever hopeful for a treat.

and we just sit there at night, and it's quiet," says Carol. As with John's unit, Carol's unit has a front porch—just large enough for two Adirondack chairs—and a small back patio to extend living space outdoors. Her bedroom is upstairs, along with another full bath and walk-in closet.

"I'm very comfortable in this place," she says. She appreciates the neighborliness of the immediate community and the site-sensitive walkability around the central court and into town. "I can walk to the bank. I can walk to the restaurants . . . I can walk to the groomer. My church is within five minutes. I can walk everywhere," she notes. The location and the simplicity of her condo means she can spend less time in the car

and on home maintenance and more time in the community and on other interests. "The smallness of this place really attracted me because I can take care of it; it's still looks clean and lovely," she continues.

Carol's attitude is in keeping with an emerging demographic for this type of new small cottage-court development that Don Powers and his partners have observed. "The people who bought into Greene Street, as they have in all of the other cottage communities we've done now, are making a virtue of the smallness. They wouldn't have more square footage if they could," says Don.

 Carol's back patio is tucked between her unit and a neighboring fence in a small outdoor room. On warm evenings, she often entertains her daughter and son-in-law or her granddaughter and great-grandchildren there.

RETREATS

THE SAME 10 DESIGN strategies that we've seen enhance the 24 small houses portrayed in this book can also be applied to small retreats, which might serve as studios, lounges, dining spaces, or whatever you can imagine. Whether a retreat is in the backyard or farther afield on its own parcel, it can benefit from:

SITE-SENSITIVE PLACEMENT

ATTENTION TO THE THIRD DIMENSION

BORROWED DAYLIGHT AND VIEW

A BIG STATEMENT

MULTIPURPOSE SPACES

POCKETS FOR PRIVACY

BRINGING THE INDOORS OUT AND THE OUTDOORS IN

A SUCCINCT FINISH PALETTE

QUALITY MATERIALS THAT MATTER

DISTINCTIVE DETAILS

If you've been dreaming of a little place of your own in the backyard or beyond, take inspiration from the five retreats we've included in the following pages. They're each less than 500 sq. ft. The scale is small, but they exhibit the same fundamental design principles as the small houses we've looked at.

A STUDIO

SITE   3D   DAYLIGHT   BIG/SMALL   MULTI-PURPOSE   PRIVACY   IN/OUT   FINISH PALETTE   QUALITY MATERIALS   DETAILS

WHEN YOU PULL IN the long driveway to access this property, the first structure you come upon is what one of the owners describes as an "artistic jewel box." It's her art studio. "We were looking to develop an interesting shape that would lead you in," explains Jim Cappuccino, the project architect for the studio (and main house) from Hutker Architects. As you continue down the driveway toward the studio you catch a sliver of a view of Buzzards Bay straight ahead to the south and then you turn toward the house and a courtyard between it and the garage.

The studio is a trapezoid in plan and features a dramatically sloping roof that peaks over the entry to announce it and makes a big statement for a small retreat. Jim notes, "It was developed based on the principles of the main house," where a more tempered sloping roof ascends over the entry and many of the same materials are on display. Both buildings incorporate a succinct finish palette of white cedar shingles, red cedar planks on a bay (which, in the case of the studio, contains a half bath), and a zinc-coated copper roof. The materials were selected to reflect the owners' taste for wabi-sabi, a Japanese term for weathered, imperfect beauty that expresses age.

Since the studio roofing material isn't visible from the approach, and the architects wanted to emphasize the

 From the lower yard, the studio interior is partially visible through the glass reflection of the bay and the house. The blank western wall funnels the view to the water from the approach and is a quiet backdrop for a new tree and the seasonal meadow.

Architect: Hutker Architects
Marion, Mass.
268 sq. ft.

The lofty roof and zinc-coated copper corner are prominent at the entry. "The setting was so appropriate because it's under the canopy of those trees along the edge where you can't see the adjacent neighbor, so it was also a private area," remarks architect Jim Cappuccino.

 From her studio desk, the owner paints with acrylics and draws with pastels. The concrete floor, buffed to turn a pewter color, recalls the concrete floors in the house. A long, narrow awning window faces the greenery of the skip laurel hedge to the east.

 The roof drops to around 7 ft. at its lowest point, compressing and intensifying the water view. Low horizontal hopper windows provide ventilation, while the big picture window offers an unobstructed view of the water, lawn, and part of the house.

projecting corner that defines both the edge of the entrance and view corridor between structures, the distinctive corner is clad in the same zinc-coated copper that's on the roof of the house. "What is beautiful about that zinc-coated copper, too, is that it takes on some of the same weathering patterns as the wood on the house," says Jim. Also prominent is a generous overhang that wraps the studio to buffer southern light on the rear glass wall.

Once you step inside, "there's a forced perspective, in a sense, straight out to that water view," Jim explains. A north-facing window, common to many artists' studios, wasn't a priority for this artist owner. "I obviously wanted to maximize my view," she notes, and to bring the indoors out and the out-doors in. (The large window faces south.) When she's paint-ing in the studio, it's mostly in the morning when the studio is lit with light filtered through the skip laurel hedge to the east and before the harsher light of midday. She says that she paints primarily for peace of mind, and it's hard to imagine a more peaceful spot for her to practice her craft.

A MEDITATIVE RETREAT

SITE   3D   DAYLIGHT   BIG/SMALL   MULTI-PURPOSE   PRIVACY   IN/OUT   FINISH PALETTE   QUALITY MATERIALS

WHEN IT COMES down to it, architecture is composed of physical materials: wood, concrete, metal, and glass. Yet we typically ask it to be so much more. Eric Fier certainly did. After his daughter's years-long struggle with Tay-Sachs disease, Eric began to conceive of a meditative space in his backyard in Atlanta that would reflect his journey with his daughter, which was one of "infinite depth within the smallest of footprints," in his words. He engaged architect Bryan Russell to help him translate "a soul-informed space" into a small contemporary retreat for reflecting, reading, writing, and napping.

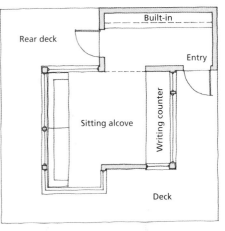

The bench memorial to Rachaeli, to the right in the foreground, provides a pocket for privacy off the slate-chip path en route to Eric's backyard retreat. A large overhanging standing-seam metal roof provides shade and shelter from rain while making a big statement on a small cypress-clad retreat.

Architect: Bryan Russell of Dencity
Atlanta, Ga.
450 sq. ft.

The back door, maple built-in cabinet, and polished concrete floor are visible beyond the concrete writing counter. Eric carefully chose objects to display, noting that "Each item that you place in such a small space carries a level of significance with it."

Placed toward the rear of his yard for more privacy, the retreat anchors what has gradually evolved into a Zen-like site-sensitive garden behind Eric's mostly brick, somewhat conventional house. "We actually tried to make the new studio blend more with nature than it did with the existing house," says Bryan. When you open the gate to the backyard, you are instantly transported into a different world. Set atop a square deck of cypress, the retreat's plan pushes and pulls

beneath a simple overhanging shed roof that's lower toward the house for privacy from the second-floor bedrooms and rises toward the view of trees to the rear. A cypress guard rail, bounding a small rectangular roof deck, pops above the roof plane and matches the walls below.

You enter the retreat from the southeast into a transitional flat-ceiling space lined with built-in display shelves and base cabinets and wind your way into either the multipurpose

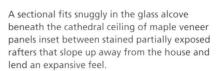

A sectional fits snuggly in the glass alcove beneath the cathedral ceiling of maple veneer panels inset between stained partially exposed rafters that slope up away from the house and lend an expansive feel.

Beyond the glassed-in sitting area hangs a chair beneath the roof overhang in a pocket for privacy off the back of the retreat. This is a favorite spot where Eric enjoys quiet Saturday mornings with a cup of coffee.

 A steel ladder climbs the back of the retreat to a small rooftop nest. "I like the fact that I have to inconvenience myself slightly to access that vantage point," says Eric.

lounging and writing space beneath a soaring cathedral ceiling or out to a private mini rear deck where a chair hangs from the eaves offering a pocket for privacy. Large panes of field-set glass surround the southwest-facing sitting alcove and share daylight with the entry and writing areas, while significant overhangs on the roof, which make a big statement, shield them from harsh afternoon sun. A writing counter acts as a pocket for privacy if others are lounging nearby, which is rare because the retreat is very much Eric's own personal space. Narrow horizontal windows just above the height of the writing surface provide Eric with a peek of the yard without posing too much of a distraction.

Quality materials, like cypress, are featured prominently and provide a warm contrast to polished concrete on the floor and the cast-in-place writing counter. Bryan specified a unique treatment for the exterior cypress rain-screen siding, which has roots in a Japanese technique called shou-sugi-ban. It involves blackening the wood with a blowtorch and scraping back the charring to a desired durable finish that is ultimately very rot and pest resistant.

The rooftop deck is accessed from the rear via a vertical steel ladder. "I like having a second vantage point," says Eric. From the "nest," as Eric calls it, he overlooks the garden and a fountain bench that memorializes his daughter, Rachaeli, who at age nine passed away during the construction of the retreat. Today, outside and inside Eric's multifaceted small backyard retreat there are ample opportunities for deep reflection on subjects small and infinite.

GARDEN ROOM GARAGE

SITE 3D DAYLIGHT BIG/SMALL MULTI-PURPOSE PRIVACY IN/OUT FINISH PALETTE QUALITY MATERIALS

SANDI COOK AND I used to work together. One day at the office, we got on a kick about wanting dining pavilions in our backyards. Another day, a group of us batted around ideas about opening a design café. On another day, we dreamed up implausible names for future design businesses. It was all in good fun, and it all seemed somewhat detached from reality—until a couple of years later when Sandi and her husband, John Greci, retained me as their architect to design a backyard pavilion for them in Manchester-by-the-Sea, Mass.

Architect: Katie Hutchison Studio
Manchester-by-the-Sea, Mass.
216 sq. ft.

 The red barnlike doors match the color of the nearby house, and alternating shingle courses above the doors play off the staggered shingle coursing detail on the house. "If you had the front doors open, you had to expect a visitor," laughs Sandi who remembers that when the weather was nice, passersby would often wander down the driveway for a look.

 With the glass sliders all the way open, exposed premium-grade pine studs and shiplap pine sheathing provide a warm backdrop for the casual Caribbean lounging decor.

It wasn't meant to be so much a dining pavilion as an outdoor entertaining space that could double as an off-season one-car garage. We located it a little closer to the street than the sad, rusting metal garage it replaced (to relieve a nonconformity to the rear), and we matched the old garage's 12-ft. by 18-ft. footprint. We decided a small barnlike gabled structure with a loft on the far end would speak to the New England vernacular of their American foursquare home.

In keeping with the barn aesthetic, we designed oversize barnlike swinging doors for the front and hefty sliding doors for the garden side. The custom wood and glass sliding doors store completely clear of the door opening, inviting the adjacent patio indoors and the garden room outdoors. Shingle brackets on the front flare to conceal the ends of double overhead tracks for the sliding doors. High hopper windows on the neighbors' side of the garage provide daylight and ventilation while preserving privacy. Large double-hung windows look out the rear toward a backyard stream. A galvanized corrugated steel roof completes the agrarian look.

Because Sandi and John enjoy the occasional jaunt to St. Barts, they opted to furnish the seasonal interior with a Caribbean flair. "Of course, down there, everything opens to the outdoors, too," notes Sandi. She and John have since moved to another property, but they found the garden room

 Sandi relaxes on the daybed draped with mosquito netting reminiscent of cabanas on St. Barts. A stone-dust floor, edged with Belgian block and sporting a sisal rug, complements the dual uses of the space.

 Because the sliding glass doors are on two overhead tracks they can be opened in any combination to filter sound, wind, or the degree of enclosure.

was a great place to enjoy the yard, take naps, and listen to the sounds of summer. "It really was very private for that neighborhood. The houses are really tight; there are a lot of kids around, and it gave us what felt like an enclosure but was not very enclosed," Sandi adds.

In the winter, they stored their furnishings in their adjacent basement and drove their 1986 VW Westfalia Camper in for safe keeping. The camper's sliding doors opened on the same side as the sliding doors in the garden room/garage "like a cabana within a cabana," says Sandi. It proved to be a versatile little building. Maybe even more fun than a dining pavilion.

SWAMP HUT

SITE | 3D | DAYLIGHT | BIG/SMALL | MULTI-PURPOSE | PRIVACY | IN/OUT | FINISH PALETTE

ARCHITECTS KEITH MOSKOW and Robert Linn designed this unusual retreat to tread lightly on swampland in Newton, Mass. According to Keith, "It was built as an experimental project" that the office would be able to enjoy as a nearby retreat unexpectedly tucked into a swamp habitat.

The plan is simple. Four 8-ft. by 12-ft. huts, positioned on the compass points, provide a protective enclosure surrounding a 14-ft. by 14-ft. central square deck. "It's very small square footage, but it feels quite a bit larger because you're looking through the corners, and you have that big outdoor room in the middle," says Keith. The northernmost structure, the most enclosing, is the cleansing/wet hut—think of it as the camping version of a kitchen/bathroom. The eastern and western structures are the sleeping huts, which

 Perched on wooden piers, the huts appear to float above the swampland. The south-facing table hut projects the highest above the sloping grade and features gable-end framing and a ridge, but no roof.

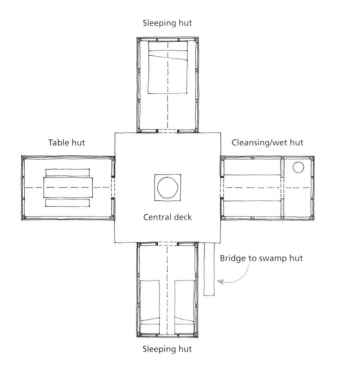

Sleeping hut

Table hut

Cleansing/wet hut

Central deck

Bridge to swamp hut

Sleeping hut

Architect: Moskow Linn Architects
Newton, Mass.
384 sq. ft.

are less enclosing. And the least enclosing southern structure is the table hut, where you might enjoy a meal, a game, or a book. The open square space in the middle is primarily formed by the faces of the four huts. Together, the huts look upon themselves and create a site-sensitive multipurpose outdoor room in their midst, bringing the indoors out and the outdoors in, while borrowing view and daylight and establishing four independent pockets for privacy.

The surprisingly tall peaked huts are simply framed and sized to minimize cuts and waste. The plate height of the low surrounding wall is 3 ft. The trusses, which were prefabricated and carried into the site, are 12 ft. high. "The idea was to create outdoor space that would be as important as indoor space, and so having a very high facade (they're very skinny) there, in a sense, made the four walls of the outdoor room," explains Keith. The most enclosing cleansing/wet hut has

You approach the huts from the northeast, where the grade is higher, and slide between the aluminum-paneled cleansing/wet hut and the translucent-paneled eastern sleeping hut.

The square windows in the gable ends of the sleeping huts frame views of nature, and the translucent panels glow with soft light, which is easy on waking eyes.

The table hut is the most open of the huts because it's a gathering space. The table and benches were made from construction scraps to minimize waste.

aluminum panels in the roof and gable end walls; it features a toilet and prep counters. All water, food, and supplies are carried in on foot, and all waste is carried out. The slightly less enclosing sleeping huts have translucent fiberglass panels in the roof and gable end walls; they house cots. The table hut has no roofing and only framing in the gable ends and the ridge across. A raised copper fire drum occupies the middle of the open deck outdoor room and has proven the ideal spot to cook marshmallows and hot dogs.

 The central fire drum can be enjoyed by folks on the deck or within the pockets for privacy that the separate huts offer. All the furnishings are lightweight and easily transportable.

THE SWISS ARMY KNIFE OF RETREATS

  SITE   3D DAYLIGHT BIG/SMALL MULTI-PURPOSE   PRIVACY   IN/OUT   FINISH PALETTE QUALITY MATERIALS   DETAILS

THIS SMALL RETREAT on Vashon Island, Wash., designed by Seth Grizzle and Jonathan Junker of the conceptual design firm Graypants is chock-full of inventive details that are space-saving multipurpose solutions. It can "do anything and nothing; it's kind of a Swiss army knife," says Seth. Built in place of a former garage at the owners' vacation property, it can function as a place to host a party, read a book, dine, house a guest, meditate, perform, and even store a vehicle.

Designers: Seth Grizzle and Jonathan Junker of Graypants
Vashon Island, Wash.
440 sq. ft.

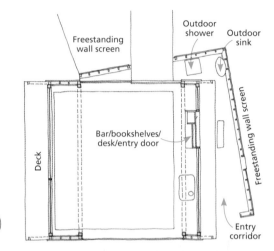

Freestanding wall screen

Outdoor shower

Outdoor sink

Deck

Bar/bookshelves/desk/entry door

Freestanding wall screen

Entry corridor

 Overlooking Puget Sound, the retreat glows like a lantern at dusk. To the right, a stepping-stone path in a pocket for privacy between the gabled retreat and the wall screen, constructed from materials reclaimed from the original garage, leads to the entry and beyond to an outdoor salvaged sink (and outdoor shower around the corner).

 A Corian cabinet housing a small bar, bookshelves, and desk also serves as a sliding entry door, packing a lot of function into a small object, which frees up space in the small retreat. The reclaimed boards of the exterior wall screen are visible through the glass wall of the new retreat.

The owners asked Seth and Jonathan to create a small space that would capture a memory of the former garage—in which they once hosted a memorable Thanksgiving—while creating something new that would celebrate the waterfront site and serve multiple functions. Seth and Jonathan responded with a design that used the materials of the former garage to create two freestanding walls that meet at a corner on the footprint of the former garage and act as a screen of sorts, from the inland east side of the property and the neighbors to the north, for a new small, mostly glass, gabled structure. They pulled the new structure forward from the corner screening walls and cranked it slightly while cantilevering it toward the views of the seascape through the glass walls.

The spaces in between the reclaimed garage wall screens and the new retreat serve as unusual pockets for privacy in the form of an entry corridor on the east side and outdoor partial bathroom on the north side. From within the pristine new 440-sq.-ft. structure, the old garage walls act as a backdrop that contributes rich texture, some privacy, and the story of what came before.

 Floor panels fold to create lounge seating positioned to take in the view, or alternatively, fold away to reveal recessed elongated twin beds. Open, cedar, ladder-like framing surrounding the waterside deck filters sunlight.

To accommodate multiple functions, Seth and Jonathan reimagined how some everyday objects are designed. For example, they reconceived the idea of what a door is and how we interact with it. They created an entry door out of a sliding Corian cabinet that can also serve multiple purposes as a bar, bookshelf, and desk. They also reimagined the nature of built-in furnishings by devising distinctive folding floor panels that can serve as lounge chairs or can be opened in combination to reveal two recessed elongated twin beds with a floor storage compartment in between. They even reappraised the idea of what a finish wall surface might be. The interior of the two copper-clad ribbons that wrap the gable form are outfitted with removable canvas panels that provide access to the mechanical and technical components they conceal. LEDs behind the canvas panels, which picture frame them, allow the interior finish surfaces to serve as light fixtures (which are controlled by a smartphone app). "We knew we had to be really efficient and pack a lot of function into this tiny beautiful object," says Jonathan.

 LEDs behind canvas panels provide diffuse light, framing the view at dusk, and LEDs tucked into fir strips mounted to the fir roof purlins provide additional integral lighting. The full glass wall makes a big statement for a small retreat and brings the indoors out and the outdoors in.

 From the water side, the cantilevered glass gable form is striking. "We wanted it to feel mighty even though it's small, and we were able to accomplish that through a simple gable form," notes Seth. The glass roof supported by structural purlins, which also provide some shading, invite the sky into the retreat and the retreat up to the sky.

CREDITS

ACKNOWLEDGMENTS

PHOTOGRAPHER: Katie Hutchison

INTRODUCTION (pp. 2-13)

ARCHITECT: Gale Goff Architect, Newport and Little Compton, RI; www.galegoff.com (p. 11, bottom)

PHOTOGRAPHERS: Susan Teare (pp. 2-5; 8, top; 9; 10), Ken Gutmaker (pp. 6-7; 8, bottom; 11, top; 13), Howard Chu (p. 11, bottom), Undine Pröhl (p. 12)

BY THE WATER

HERON COTTAGE (cover, pp. 16-21)

ARCHITECT: Will Winkelman, Winkelman Architecture, Portland, ME; www.winkarch.com

PHOTOGRAPHER: Susan Teare

MODERN VERNACULAR (pp. 22-28)

ARCHITECT: MacKay-Lyons Sweetapple Architects, Halifax, Nova Scotia, Canada; www.mlsarchitects.ca

PHOTOGRAPHER: William Green

LOW PROFILE, BOLD PRESENCE (pp. 14-15; 29-35)

ARCHITECT: Eggleston/Farkas Architects, Seattle, WA; www.eggfarkarch.com

PHOTOGRAPHER: Ken Gutmaker

ISLAND CHARM (pp. 36-43)

DESIGNER: Sandra Cook, Tiro Design and Construction LLC, Beverly, MA; and Joan Young

PHOTOGRAPHER: Jo-Ann Richards, Works Photography

CAPE COD CASUAL (pp. 44-49)

ARCHITECT: Estes/Twombly Architects, Newport, RI; www.estestwombly.com

PHOTOGRAPHER: Susan Teare

SETTLED INTO THE LANDSCAPE (pp. i, 50-55)

ARCHITECT: Will Winkelman and Eric Sokol, Winkelman Architecture, Portland, ME; www.winkarch.com

PHOTOGRAPHER: Susan Teare

IN THE COUNTRY

RESIDENT GUESTHOUSE (pp. 58-64)

ARCHITECT: John Carney, Carney Logan Burke Architects, Jackson, WY; www.clbarchitects.com

PHOTOGRAPHER: Ken Gutmaker

PASSION FOR PASSIVE (pp. 65-72)

ARCHITECT: Matthew O'Malia, GO Logic LLC, Belfast, ME; www.gologic.us

PHOTOGRAPHER: Brian Vanden Brink

BARNHOUSE MODERN (pp. 56-57; 73-79)

ARCHITECT: DeForest Architects, Seattle, WA, and Tahoe, CA; www.deforestarchitects.com

PHOTOGRAPHERS: Farshid Assassi (pp. 56-57; 73; 75; 76; 77, top; 79); John DeForest (p. 74); Mark Mahaney (p. 77, bottom; 78)

LONGHOUSE (pp. 80-87)

ARCHITECT: Eric Reinholdt, 30x40 Design Workshop, Mount Desert, ME; www.thirtybyforty.com

PHOTOGRAPHER: Susan Teare

PREFAB GLASS HOUSE (pp. 88-95)

ARCHITECT: Taalman Koch Architecture, Los Angeles, CA; www.taalmankoch.com

PHOTOGRAPHER: Undine Pröhl

THE 20K HOUSE (pp. 96-103)

DESIGNER: Auburn University Rural Studio Outreach Program, Newbern, AL; www.ruralstudio.org

PHOTOGRAPHER: Tim Hursley (except p. 99, bottom: Danny Wicke)

IN THE VILLAGE

WHITE ON WHITE (pp. 106-112)
ARCHITECT: Priestley + Associates Architecture, Rockport, ME; www.ppaarch.com
PHOTOGRAPHER: Susan Teare

THE WEST WING (pp. 113-118)
ARCHITECT: Ned White, McCoppin Studios, San Francisco, CA, and Salt Lake City, UT; www.mccoppin.com
PHOTOGRAPHER: Ken Gutmaker

PUBLIC–PRIVATE SWAP (pp. 104-105; 119-125)
ARCHITECT: Allen Architecture, Fort Worth, TX; www.allenarc.com
PHOTOGRAPHER: Brian McWeeney

AN ARTIST'S HOUSE (pp. 126-131)
DESIGNER: Pat Warwick, Warren, RI
PHOTOGRAPHER: Susan Teare

TOWER HOUSE (pp. 132-139)
ARCHITECT: Matt Kirkpatrick, Design for Occupancy, Portland, OR; www.designforoccupancy.net
PHOTOGRAPHER: Ken Gutmaker

CALIFORNIA COMPOUND (pp. 140-147)
INTERIOR DESIGNER/LANDSCAPE PLANNER: Josh Heiser, O'donnell Lane, LLC, Sonoma, CA; www.odonnell-lane.com
PHOTOGRAPHER: Ken Gutmaker

IN TOWN

A NARROW HOUSE (pp. 150-156)
ARCHITECT: Mowery Marsh Architects LLC, Hoboken, NJ; www.mowerymarsh.com
PHOTOGRAPHER: Susan Teare

FAMILY ADU (pp. ii, 157-163)
ARCHITECT: Steven Routon Architect / LLC, Clatskanie, OR
PHOTOGRAPHER: Ken Gutmaker

VICTORIAN MODERN (pp. 164-170)
ARCHITECT: Ted Chapin, Provincetown, MA
PHOTOGRAPHER: Susan Teare

THE SAMUEL NOAKES HOUSE ANEW (pp. 171-179)
ARCHITECT: Reader & Swartz Architects, P.C., Winchester, VA; www.readerswartz.com
PHOTOGRAPHERS: Nathan Webb (pp. 171-174; 179); Greg Hadley (pp. 175-178)

EASTIE VERSATILITY (pp. 148-149; 180-186)
ARCHITECT: Lyle Bradley, East Boston, MA
PHOTOGRAPHER: Susan Teare

NEW ENGLAND COTTAGE COURT (pp. 187-195)
ARCHITECT: Union Studio, Providence, RI; www.unionstudioarch.com
PHOTOGRAPHER: Susan Teare

RETREATS

A STUDIO (pp. 198-200)
ARCHITECT: Hutker Architects, Falmouth, MA; www.hutkerarchitects.com
PHOTOGRAPHER: Susan Teare

A MEDITATIVE RETREAT (pp. 201-204)
ARCHITECT: Bryan Russell, Dencity, Atlanta, GA; www.dencity.us
LANDSCAPE ARCHITECT: CORE Landscape Group, Atlanta, GA; www.coreatlanta.com.
PHOTOGRAPHER: Fredrik Brauer (except p. 202, Eric Fier)

GARDEN ROOM GARAGE (pp. 205-207)
ARCHITECT: Katie Hutchison Studio, Warren, RI; www.katiehutchison.com
PHOTOGRAPHER: Katie Hutchison

SWAMP HUT (pp. 208-211)
ARCHITECT: Moskow Linn Architects, Boston, MA; www.moskowlinn.com
PHOTOGRAPHER: Moskow Linn Architects

THE SWISS ARMY KNIFE OF RETREATS (pp. 196-197; 212-215)
ARCHITECT: Seth Grizzle and Jonathan Junker, Graypants, Seattle, WA; www.graypants.com
PHOTOGRAPHER: Amos Morgan

If you like this book, you'll love *Fine Homebuilding*.